Contents

Figures

Tables

Dear Colleagues,

As law enforcement agencies throughout the nation continue to face challenges brought about by the current economic changes, it is increasingly important that law enforcement practitioners and our communities work together to ensure the safety of the public. The core mission of the United States Department of Justice (USDOJ) is the protection of the American people, and the law enforcement community plays an integral role in the advancement of this mission. As a component of the Justice Department, the COPS Office is committed to acting as the voice for state and local law enforcement agencies within the federal government. We believe that the changes that have been occurring across the country are going to continue to have a serious impact on the way American police agencies operate in the years to come.

Central to the philosophy of community policing is the achievement and advancement of public safety by building relationships and solving problems on a local, neighborhood level. As police departments across the nation face budget cuts, and are therefore limited in resources and staffing levels, community policing strategies are essential to maintaining effective public safety services within this changing economy.

The Department of Justice is determined to help build the framework necessary to enable our law enforcement partners to make the most of these limited resources and to promote promising and effective public safety efforts. In advancing these goals, the COPS Office recently awarded more than $240 million in new grants that supported the hiring and retention of more than 1,000 officers in 238 agencies and municipalities across the country. These funding opportunities helped support local departments to increase the total number of staff; enhance their relationship with the community; and directly address the public safety concerns facing their communities.

This report also reflects our commitment to assisting local law enforcement agencies thrive in the current economy. To date, it is also the first federal analysis that examines the impact the economy has had on the law enforcement community. It is our goal to continue to examine these issues so that we may provide the best available resources, information, and guidance to the field to assist police in the development of sustainable policies and procedures that will help shape the new reality in American policing.

Sincerely,

Bernard K. Melekian, Director
Office of Community Oriented Policing Services

About the COPS Office

The Office of Community Oriented Policing Services (the COPS Office) is the component of the U.S. Department of Justice responsible for advancing the practice of community policing by the nation's state, local, and tribal law enforcement agencies through information and grant resources. The community policing philosophy promotes organizational strategies that support the systematic use of partnerships and problem-solving techniques to proactively address the immediate conditions that give rise to public safety issues such as crime, social disorder, and fear of crime. In its simplest form, community policing is about building relationships and solving problems.

The COPS Office awards grants to state, local, and tribal law enforcement agencies to hire and train community policing professionals, acquire and deploy cutting-edge crime-fighting technologies, and develop and test innovative policing strategies. The COPS Office funding also provides training and technical assistance to community members and local government leaders and all levels of law enforcement.

Since 1994, the COPS Office has invested more than $16 billion to add community policing officers to the nation's streets, enhance crime fighting technology, support crime prevention initiatives, and provide training and technical assistance to help advance community policing. More than 500,000 law enforcement personnel, community members, and government leaders have been trained through COPS Office-funded training organizations.

The COPS Office has produced more than 1,000 information products—and distributed more than 2 million publications—including Problem Oriented Policing Guides, Grant Owner's Manuals, fact sheets, best practices, and curricula. And in 2010, the COPS Office participated in 45 law enforcement and public-safety conferences in 25 states in order to maximize the exposure and distribution of these knowledge products. More than 500 of those products, along with other products covering a wide area of community policing topics—from school and campus safety to gang violence—are currently available, at no cost, through its online Resource Information Center at www.cops.usdoj.gov. More than 2 million copies have been downloaded in FY2010 alone. The easy to navigate and up to date website is also the grant application portal, providing access to online application forms.

Acknowledgments

This report was developed by the Research & Development Division, in the Community Policing Advancement Directorate—specifically through the efforts of Jessica Mansourian, John Markovic, Deborah Spence, and Mora Fiedler.

U.S. Department of Justice
Office of Community Oriented Policing Services (the COPS Office)
Community Policing Advancement Directorate
Research & Development Division

Introduction

The economic downturn of the past several years has been devastating to local economies and, by extension, their local law enforcement agencies. According to a report by the National Institute of Justice, the United States is currently experiencing the 10th economic decline since World War II (Wiseman 2011). The impact of this downturn will result in a change of how law enforcement services are delivered. As has been discussed by the COPS Office Director, Bernard Melekian, in a series of recent articles published in the *Community Policing Dispatch*, expectations will not be lowered just because an agency now has fewer officers, or because the budget is limited. Simply doing less while waiting for local budgets to recover to pre-2008 levels is not a viable option. Faced with a dramatic budget contraction, law enforcement leaders need to start identifying different ways to deliver police services and, perhaps more importantly, articulate what the new public safety models will look like to their communities (Melekian 2011a). The effects of the economic downturn on law enforcement agencies may be felt for the next 5–10 years, or worse, permanently. The permanence of this change will be driven not just by the economy, but by the local government officials determining that allocating 30–50 percent of their general fund budgets for public safety costs is no longer a fiscal possibility (Melekian 2011b).

While some people see signs that the economy is beginning to recover on the national level, most economists agree that local jurisdictions are still in decline and will continue to be so, at least in the short term. County and municipal budgets tend to lag behind the general economy and continuing foreclosures are slowing the recovery of property tax revenues, which are the backbone of local agency funding. Faced with these budget realities, the current model for service delivery—which has been with us for the last 50 years—is already starting to change, and will be forced to continue to change dramatically and rapidly in the next 3–5 years. As articulated in the June edition of the *Community Policing Dispatch*, Director Melekian discusses the need for a change in delivery of police services from a mid-20th century model to a more forward-looking 21st century model. He explains:

> *Police service delivery can be categorized into three tiers. The first tier, emergency response, is not going to change. Tier two is non-emergency response; where officers respond to calls after the fact, primarily to collect the information and statements necessary to produce reports. These calls, while an important service, do not require rapid response—the business has already been vandalized, the bike already stolen. Tier three deals with quality of life issues, such as crime prevention efforts or traffic management duties. They help make our communities better places to live, but they are proactive and ongoing activities. The second and third tiers of police service delivery have always competed for staffing and financial resources, but as local budgets constrict, that competition becomes fiercer. The public expects that both tiers are addressed, and agencies with shrinking payrolls are faced with finding new ways to make sure that can happen (Melekian 2011c).*

Faced with these dramatic budget contractions, law enforcement leaders have begun identifying the most cost conscious ways to deliver police services, and developing a new model of policing that will ensure that communities continue to receive the quality police protection they are entitled to. In a 2011 survey of police chiefs conducted by the International Association of Chiefs of Police (IACP), 94 percent of respondents agreed that they were seeing "a new reality in American policing developing" (IACP 2011).

Police agencies are some of the hardest hit by the current economic climate. Curtailing revenues nationwide have forced local governments to make cuts in spending across the board, which includes public safety operating budgets. While budget cuts threaten the jobs of law enforcement officers, the duties and responsibilities to ensure public safety remain.

However, to date, there has been no systematic way of measuring the impact the economic downturn has had on police agencies across the country. This report intends to delve into the existing information, research the ways in which law enforcement agencies have been affected, and examine the ways they have responded.

The following surveys, publications, and data sets were used in this report in order to analyze how the economic downturn has affected staffing at police agencies, delivery of services, and organizational management.

The Recession Continues: An Economic Status Survey of Counties

In February 2011 the National Association of Counties (NACo) published a report titled, *The Recession Continues: An Economic Status Survey of Counties*, which outlined the results of a survey of 500 counties (across population size) as a means to determine the impact that the declining economy was having on county budgets, and the ways in which these counties were reacting to the challenge of lower revenues. The results of the study showed that counties were cutting services and personnel, as well as making across-the-board cuts to budgets, in order to address shortfalls. The data are different than what was found from previous surveys, where counties indicated they were using pay and hiring freezes to deal with the economic downturn. As the shape of the economy has gradually worsened, more counties have turned to furloughs and layoffs, with 53 percent of counties working with fewer staff in FY2011 than in FY2010 (Byers 2011).

National Survey of County Elected Officials – Looking for the Light at the End of the Tunnel: A National Survey of County Elected Officials on the Economy, Budgets, and Politics

In 2011 a survey developed by the Carl Vinson Institute of Government, in partnership with NACo, polled a random sample of 508 county officials on issues related to the economy, budgets, and politics. Overall, the study found that while many elected county officials still rate the national economy as poor, there appears to be a slightly more optimistic opinion than what was found in the 2010 study (Clark 2011).

Policing in the 21st Century: Preliminary Survey Results

As a part of President Mark A. Marshall's Policing in the 21st Century Initiative, IACP conducted a number of surveys and held roundtable discussions with over 400 law enforcement leaders to discuss the impact that the new economy is having on the field. These efforts were spearheaded by IACP's Research Division, working in partnership with IACP's Division of State Associations of Chiefs of Police, Division of State and Provincial Police, the Indian Country Section, and Mid-Size Cities Section (IACP 2011). Results of the study provide insight into ways in which national police agencies are responding to the effects of the economic climate on their agency operations.

Major Cities Chiefs Association (MCCA) Survey

In 2011 the Major Cities Chiefs Association surveyed 23 major city departments to discuss the economic challenges they faced in light of the current economy (MCCA 2011). The results demonstrate some of the trends that are being experienced in police agencies across the nation as a result of reductions to operating budgets.

Is the Economic Downturn Fundamentally Changing How We Police?

This is the 16th report in the "Critical Issues in Policing Series" that the Police Executive Research Forum (PERF) has developed in order to provide timely information and guidance on a number of difficult issues that police agencies have faced over the years. The report highlights findings from a survey conducted in 2010 of 608 police agencies focusing on the current economic challenges their departments are facing, and what the agencies have done in order to confront such challenges (PERF 2010).

State of America's Cities Survey on Jobs and the Economy

The *State of America's Cities* is an annual survey of municipal officials that has been conducted for almost 25 years by The National League of Cities (NLC). The 2010 survey yielded 349 respondents consisting of local officials from various cities nationwide. The data from the survey provide insight into the effects of declining fiscal and economic conditions on American cities (McFarland 2010).

City Fiscal Conditions in 2010

The *City Fiscal Conditions Survey* is a national survey of city financial officers throughout the United States. The survey yielded 338 respondents from cities of different population sizes, and produced information on the current fiscal state of the nation's cities and the struggles cities face while managing rapidly declining revenues (Hoene and Pagano 2010).

Law Enforcement Management and Administrative Statistics (LEMAS)

The Department of Justice Bureau of Justice Statistics (BJS) is the United States' primary source of criminal justice statistics. Every "3 to 4 years, LEMAS collects data from over 3,000 state and local law enforcement agencies, including all those that employ 100 or more sworn officers" as well as "a nationally representative sample of smaller agencies. Data are obtained on the organization and administration of police and sheriffs' departments, including agency responsibilities, operating expenditures, job functions of sworn and civilian employees, officer salaries and special pay, demographic characteristics of officers, weapons and armor policies, education and training requirements, computers and information systems, vehicles, special units, and community policing activities" (LEMAS 2011).

Census of State and Local Law Enforcement Agencies (CSLLEA)

In conjunction with the LEMAS data discussed above, BJS also conducts a census every 4 years of publicly funded law enforcement agencies with one or more full-time-equivalent sworn staff. This master list of law enforcement agencies is compiled from the previous CSLLEA census; lists provided by Peace Officer Standards and Training offices and other state agencies; and a list of agencies requesting new FBI-ORI identifiers since the previous CSLLEA. The latest CSLLEA was conducted in 2008 and included 17,985 state and local law enforcement agencies employing at least one full-time officer or the equivalent in part-time officers. The CSLLEA represents the sampling universe from which the LEMAS survey is drawn. Data collected as part of the CSLLEA include number of sworn personnel, number of civilian personnel, and agency-type category (CSLLEA 2011). CSLLEA data are recognized as the most definitive counts of law enforcement agency personnel operating with local, state, and tribal funding.

COPS Hiring Program (CHP) – Office of Community Oriented Policing Services, U.S. Department of Justice

For the last 3 years, the Department of Justice, Office of Community Oriented Policing Services (the COPS Office) has collected data from its Hiring Program applicants, including data on agency operating budgets, officer and civilian layoffs, furloughs, hiring freezes, service populations, and authorized and actual sworn force strengths. With thousands of applicants each year, the data set represents a sizeable sample of all the state, local, and tribal law enforcement agencies in this country, although it is not a random sample. For the analysis in this report, two subsets of data were used. The first subset is all the agencies that submitted a hiring program application in 2011 and who are currently staffed with at least 10 full-time officers. The second subset is those agencies that applied both in 2009 and 2011, as well as having at least 10 full-time officers. The significance of the 10 officer threshold is that while agencies of at least that size account for just 51 percent of all law enforcement agencies in this country, they employ more than 95 percent of all sworn officers. In addition, those agencies can generally be presumed to be full-service departments offering 24/7 patrol and response coverage.

Some of the CHP data used in this report will evaluate the total sample of applicants regardless of sworn force levels. These samples will be indicated as such.

News Media

Current news articles offer a way to capture the effects of the economic downturn that police agencies throughout the country are experiencing and highlight the ways in which agencies are mitigating the adverse effects of cuts to operating budgets. Within each section of this report, information from numerous media outlets helps to paint a more personal picture of how law enforcement agencies are dealing with today's challenges.

A New Method of Data Collection is Pertinent to Successful Resource Allocation

The lack of an annual and systematic data collection of law enforcement agencies nationwide poses serious challenges for the development of aggressive and productive problem-solving strategies. In order to successfully develop effective techniques to combat challenges resulting from the economic climate, it is important to have an accurate understanding of the problems that are facing police agencies as they occur. While the BJS census (CSLEAA) and survey (LEMAS) provide representative and systematic data about U.S. law enforcement agencies and staffing, they were last administered prior to the current recession. It is likely that by the time the next cycle of BJS data is available much of the economic turbulence that has occurred over the past three years will have changed yet again.

The BJS census and surveys of law enforcement agencies are methodologically robust and have enormous intrinsic value. However, the cycle by which the census and survey data are collected (every 3–4 years), as well the time lag between when the data are collected and when they are made publically available are not ideal for the types of analysis we believe are necessary for keeping on top of important trends as they emerge. The usefulness of these data sources for assessments of economic impact would be enhanced if the data were collected more often and made available in a shorter time frame. The next census and survey data for law enforcement agencies, to be conducted in 2011, will likely reveal a new reality in policing that is fundamentally different to what we have seen to date. Moreover, by the time the data is readily available (typically several years after collection) the entire state of the American economy will have changed and the immediate impacts of the recession on police agencies will have already occurred. Given the historic importance of state, local, and tribal law enforcement and their impact on the quality of life, the COPS Office feels the law enforcement community and the Department of Justice could benefit by enhancing these efforts of data collection and release by determining whether annual reports would be feasible. Even if the urgency of data collection was not underscored by the current economic crisis, a more timely collection and dissemination of data would be warranted by the new responsibilities law enforcement agencies have taken on in the last decade (i.e., homeland security, cyber crime, and greater cooperation necessitated in a more globalized society). Indeed, never has the need been more important for immediate and proactive data analysis of this kind. Federal, state, and local governments can collaboratively and effectively refocus and realign their resources to ensure the successful preservation of public safety, but their efforts will be compromised significantly if they lack up-to-date data and metrics on which to base their efforts. In summation, we encourage our colleagues at the Department of Justice to support ongoing efforts at BJS, as well as consider more frequent and timely censuses and surveys of law enforcement agencies.

The World of Policing Prior to the Great Recession

To properly assess the changes that have occurred among police agencies as a result of the economic downturn, it is important to get an idea of what police agencies looked like before.

Law Enforcement Trends Prior to the Economic Downturn

Periodically, BJS conducts two major data collection efforts. One is a census of state, local, county, and tribal law enforcement agencies (CSLLEA) and the other is a more detailed survey of approximately 3,000 state and local law enforcement agencies, including all those that employ 100 or more sworn officers and a nationally representative sample of smaller agencies (LEMAS). The most recent data are from 2008, prior to the current economic downturn (see Figure 1). The data provide an overview of the staffing numbers police agencies nationwide have maintained in the years prior to the economic downturn

Full-Time, Part-Time, and Full-Time Equivalent Sworn Officers, LEMAS and LE Census, 1986–2008

	CSLLEA 1986	LEMAS 1987	LEMAS 1990	CSLLEA 1992	LEMAS 1993	CSLLEA 1996	LEMAS 1997	CSLLEA 2000	LEMAS 2000	LEMAS 2003	CSLLEA 2004	LEMAS 2007	CSLLEA 2008
FT Sworn	496,845	510,422	547,740	562,583	581,216	618,465	648,688	661,979	656,645	683,599	680,182	700,259	704,814
PT Sworn	35,298	25,306	32,978	35,934	39,427	41,953	41,779	37,718	38,511	35,152	40,533	34,132	39,198
1/2 PT Sworn	17,649	12,653	16,489	17,967	19,714	20,977	20,889	18,859	19,256	17,576	20,267	17,066	19,599
FTE Sworn	514,494	523,075	564,229	580,550	600,930	639,441	669,577	680,838	675,901	701,175	700,449	717,325	724,413
Agencies	15,641	14,081	15,148	15,637	15,494	16,715	16,700	15,785	15,798	15,766	15,882	15,636	15,614

Figure 1. Full-Time, Part-Time, and Full-Time Equivalent sworn officers data from 1986–2008

Source: Bureau of Justice Statistics

Figure 2 (on page 8) indicates that since 1986 the number of general purpose law enforcement agencies (publicly funded law enforcement agencies with the full-time equivalent of at least one sworn officer with arrest powers) fluctuated between about 14,000 and 17,000. (This graph excludes special purpose police agencies that are included in the analysis of the BJS census, e.g., the 17,985 total agencies in 2008.)

Note: Most of the fluctuation in agencies is accounted for by smaller agencies that tend to come in and out of existence, but some may be reflective of newly formed agencies or consolidations. There is no systematic effort to track newly formed or consolidated agencies.

The Number of Law Enforcement Officers Was on a Steady Upward Climb Through 2008

As indicated in Figure 3 (on page 8), there was a steady increase in the number of full-time equivalent sworn officers employed by general purpose state and local law enforcement agencies between 1986 (N= 514,494) and 2008 (N= 724,413). This represents a 41 percent increase in sworn personnel over the entire period, although the growth was slower from 1997 on.

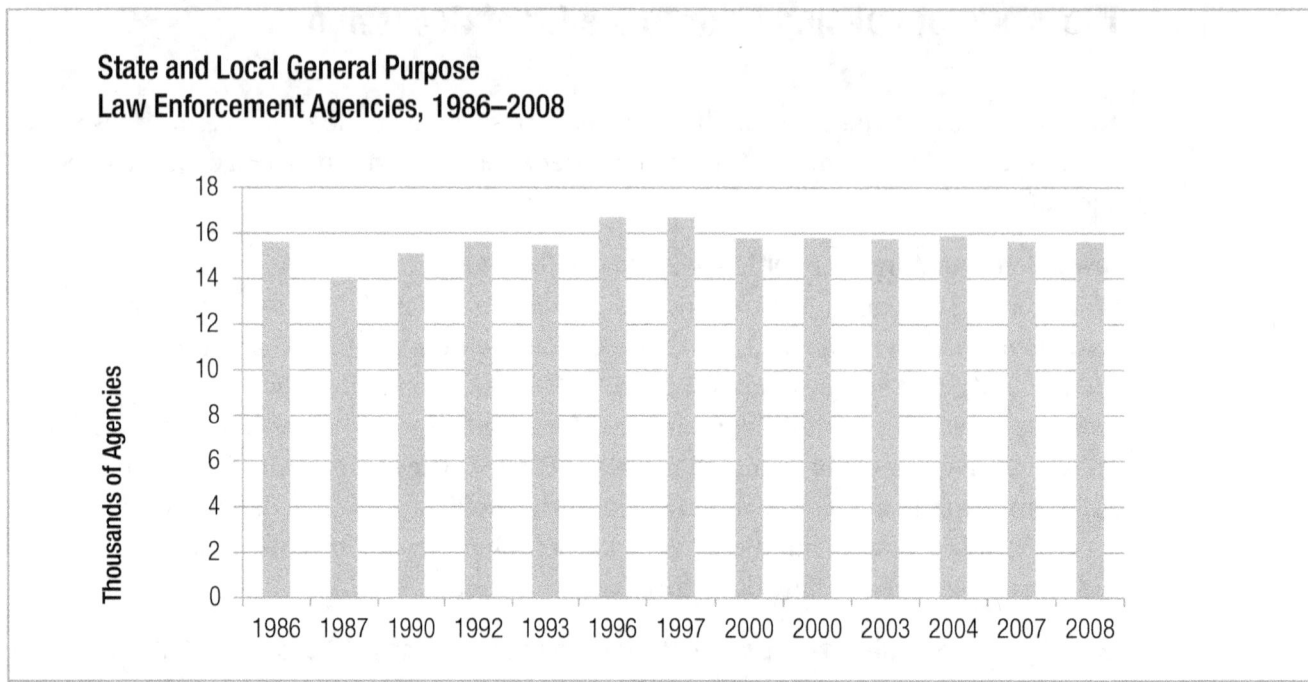

Figure 2. General purpose state and local law enforcement agencies identified by BJS Census

Source: Bureau of Justice Statistics

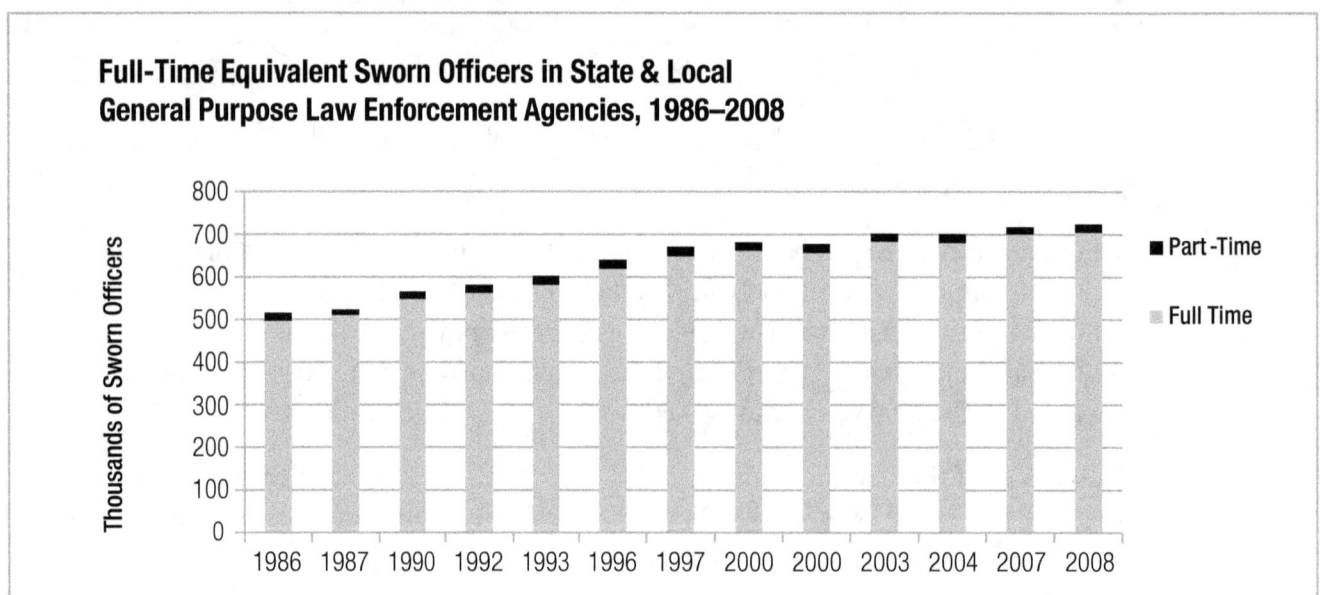

Figure 3. Full-Time Equivalent sworn officers in state and local general purpose agencies

Source: Bureau of Justice Statistics

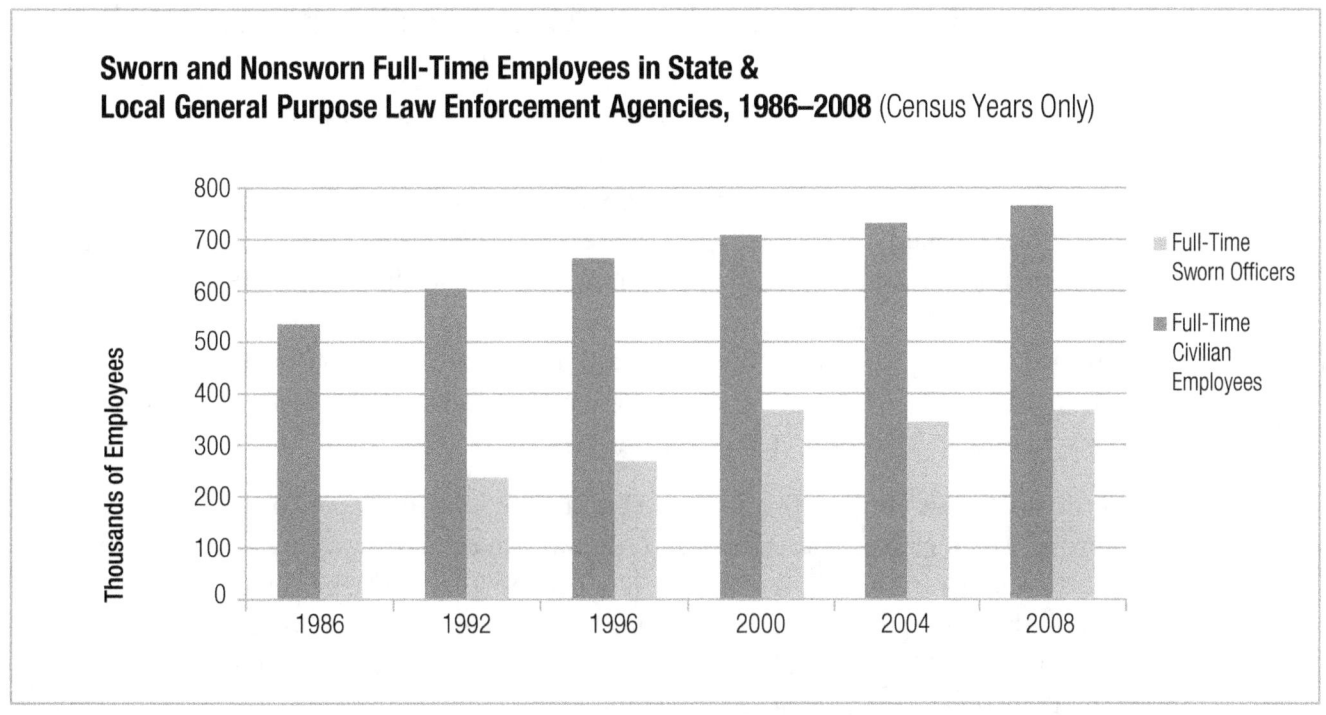

Figure 4. Full-Time Equivalent sworn officers and civilian employees in state and local general purpose agencies

Source: Bureau of Justice Statistics

Civilian Personnel Also Increased Steadily Prior to 2008

As Figure 4 indicates (based only on census years), the increase in sworn personnel was paralleled with an increase in civilian personnel. The increase in civilian personnel between 1986 and 2008 (91 percent) actually outpaced the increase in sworn personnel (41 percent). This historic data indicate a general increase in civilianization. In 2008, civilians accounted for about one-third (32.5 percent) of full-time employees in general purpose law enforcement agencies. In 1986, civilians had accounted for just over one-fourth (26.5 percent).

The preceding analysis of BJS data indicates there had been steady increase in law enforcement personnel, both sworn and civilian, between 1986 and 2008. No BJS census or survey data for law enforcement agencies have been collected since the current economic downturn. New data that are scheduled to be collected by BJS in 2011 should prove to be revealing. It will likely reveal the first ever decrease in national, state, local, and tribal law enforcement personnel since BJS began collecting data in 1986. This trend is clearly linked to the economic downturn, but what makes it more adverse is that the national population continues to grow and police have to take on new responsibilities related to homeland security, cybercrime, and modern challenges.

The Great Recession Has Changed the Face of American Policing

The economic crisis that began in 2008 has changed America in many ways. Unemployment rates have increased sharply, the stability of the housing market has collapsed, consumer spending has slowed, city revenues have lessened, and the federal deficit has reached a record level. As the fiscal conditions worsen and costs continue to escalate, many have articulated that America must learn how to "do more with less." However, when it comes to public safety, scholars and practitioners have noted that this motto is simply not a viable option. Instead, law enforcement agencies must develop ways to do things *differently*, and use the resources that are available in the most efficient and effective ways possible.

In the 2010 NLC study of the nation's city finance officers, data showed the largest downturn in revenues and cutbacks in spending in the history of the survey, with revenues declining for the fourth year in a row. Further, since city budgets tend to lag behind the national economic conditions by anywhere between 18 months to several years, the belief is that 2011 will likely result in further revenue declines and cuts in spending (Hoene and Pagano 2010).

Similar findings resulted from the 2010 NLC survey of municipal officials, in which 75 percent reported that the overall economic and fiscal conditions within their cities had worsened over the past year. Nearly a quarter of cities (22 percent) indicated that they had made cuts to public safety, which were likely to impact activities essential to the quality of life and safety of their cities, such as crime prevention and service response times (McFarland 2010).

In particular, the economic decline has severely affected law enforcement agencies' operating budgets across the nation. While there is no systematic data collection method used to gather information on how law enforcement agencies' budgets have been affected in the past few years, using the data from a number of smaller studies provides an idea of the prevalence, scope, and type of budget constraints affecting police across America.

The following data reflect local law enforcement agencies' responses to questions related to reductions in their operating budgets.

PERF Study
- Over half of the responding agencies (51 percent) reported a decrease in their budgets between fiscal years 2009 and 2010, with an average budget cut of 7 percent.
- Of the departments that experienced budget cuts in 2010, 59 percent were expecting additional cuts in FY2011 (PERF 2010).

IACP Study
- Over 85 percent of agencies reported that they were forced to reduce their budget over the last year.

- More than half of the respondents reported that they had to reduce their budgets in the prior year by 5 percent or more; a quarter had to reduce their budgets by more than 10 percent.

- These reductions were on top of the cuts that agencies already had to endure over the past several years.

- Most did not anticipate the reductions or the seriousness of the problem to end soon. In fact, 98 percent of respondents stated that they anticipated the economic impact on their agency was going to be at least "somewhat" problematic in the upcoming year.

- Over 40 percent said the coming year presented a serious or severe problem to their agency, with over one-third saying that they would have to further reduce their budgets by 10 percent or more in the coming year (IACP 2011).

MCCA Study

- Seventy-eight percent of respondents indicated that their department had experienced budget cuts, with an average budget reduction of 5.4 percent.

- Of those who experienced budget reductions, 97 percent said they had experienced flat or reduced budgets over the past 1 to 12 years.

- Forty-three percent of respondents stated they had experienced reduced/flat budgets within the last 3 years (MCCA 2011).

COPS Hiring Program (CHP)

In analyzing the budget data provided by applicants over the past 3 years (for agencies that applied both in 2009 and 2011 with a sworn staff of 10 or more) from 2009 to 2011, the average change in agency budget was an increase of only 1.75 percent. Despite this slight increase in average budget, it was found that over one third (35.7 percent) of 2011 applicants reported a budget drop of greater than 5 percent between 2009 and 2011. This is based on those 2011 applicants who provided operating budget data for both years (N= 2,701). This proportion is consistent with the findings of the PERF, IACP, and MCAA studies. During that same period, the Consumer Price Index (the generally accepted indicator of inflation) increased 1.09 percent in 2010, and then another 3.57 percent in 2011 (see Figure 5 on page 12). The cost of business rarely gets cheaper, and the costs of police services have escalated in spite of declining or stagnant operating budgets. Salaries and insurance costs—which can make up 90 percent or more of a police budget—generally increase as employees earn years of experience, making it extremely difficult for agencies to make enough cuts in other areas in order to maintain a balanced budget (Wexler 2010). Further, vehicle fuel costs have also increased dramatically in recent years, with the national average price of gasoline up 45 percent from just 5 years ago, with even higher price spikes experienced in the spring of 2008 and again earlier this year (Department of Energy 2011). All of these factors combine to put added pressure on agency operating budgets.

These data indicate that among these agencies, operating budgets that *were* fairly stagnant are now losing spending power as they fail to keep up with the rate of inflation. If operating costs continue to rise, and revenues continue to decline, law enforcement agencies will likely remain challenged to provide policing services at the levels that citizens are accustomed to receiving.

Effects on Staffing

As agencies have been pressured to make difficult decisions in light of the current fiscal conditions, many are being forced to provide the same services with fewer employees than they have in the past.

- According to a May 2010 survey conducted by the National League of Cities, 71 percent of city officials surveyed reported making cuts to personnel in order to deal with the fiscal implications of the current economic conditions. This number increased to 79 percent of survey respondents by the October report (McFarland 2010).

- A 2011 survey by the National Association of Counties found that counties are cutting services and employees, with 53 percent of counties working with fewer staff today than in FY2010 (Byers 2011).

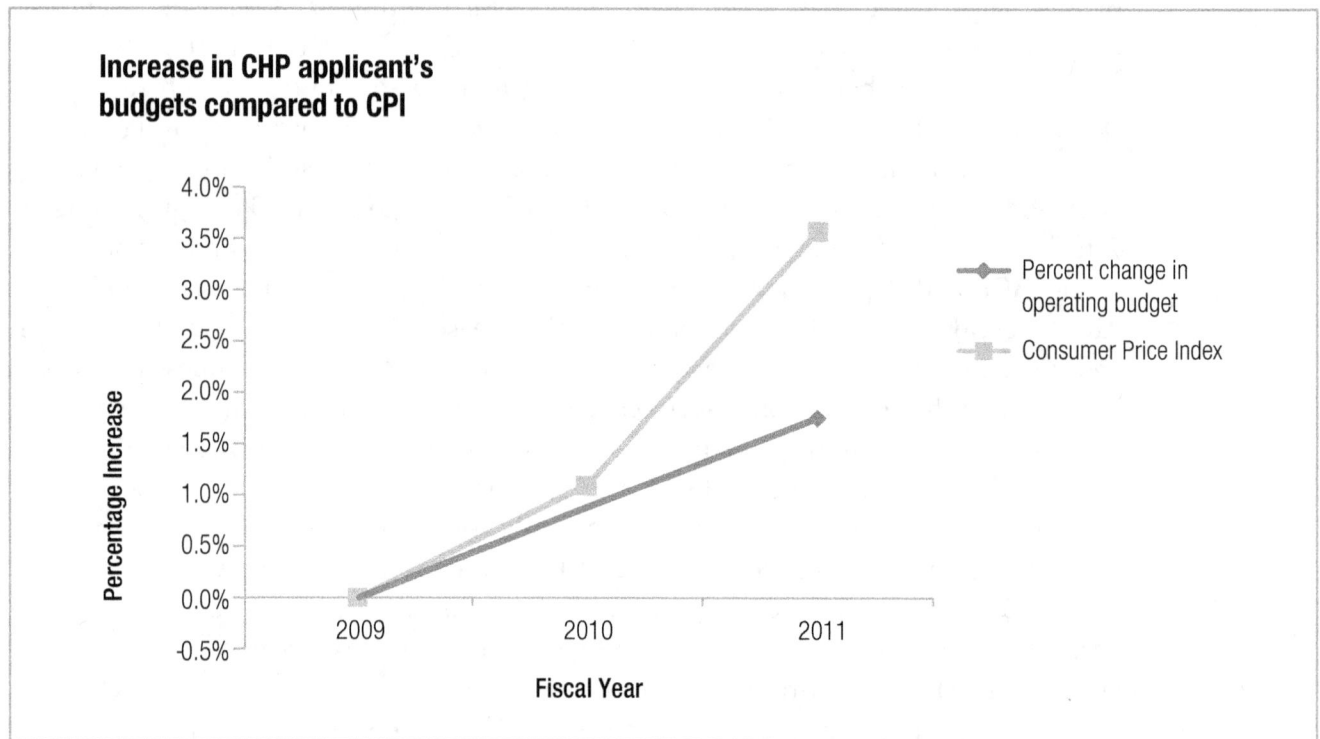

Figure 5. Average percent increase in operating budget of COPS Hiring Program applicants from 2009 and 2011 as compared to the increase in Consumer Price Index over that same time period

Source: The COPS Office

- Among respondents to the 2010 PERF study, there was a 3 percent decrease in the average number of sworn officers between FY2009 and FY2010 (PERF 2010).

Agencies have used a number of techniques to reduce their personnel costs. Layoffs, mandatory furloughs, and attrition are often the result of these budget reductions in many police agencies.

Layoffs

Currently, the data of officer positions laid off are not collected by any one agency. However, the Bureau of Justice Statistics is planning to collect the data in their 2011 LEMAS Survey. Given that the LEMAS Survey uses a stratified random sample,[1] the study should provide a reliable estimate of layoffs using weighted averages (based on the agency size stratification scheme).

So while there is no single database of layoff information, a number of smaller agencies have put together estimates regarding the number of police positions terminated as a result of budget reductions.

- The Fraternal Order of Police can directly document 4,000 layoffs, but estimates relying on less direct measurements suggest a more realistic number would be between 12,000 and 15,000 sworn officer positions lost.
- The International Association of Chiefs of Police estimate the number of law enforcement officer positions lost is 10,000.
- COPS Hiring Program data for the last 18 months estimate that 5,738 state, local, and tribal law enforcement officers have been laid off. The actual number may be as high as 10,000 if one extrapolates beyond the applicant pool to the full universe of U.S. law enforcement agencies.

Police Layoffs

IN THE NEWS:

PATERSON, NEW JERSEY POLICE DEPARTMENT laid off 125 officers on april 18, 2011. This is a quarter of their entire force. In addition, more than 30 lieutenants and sergeants were demoted to patrol. Patterson experienced a 15 percent spike in violent crime in 2010 over the 2009 level (CBS Broadcasting, Inc. 2011; Henry 2011).

FLINT, MICHIGAN – The Flint police force has been hurting since being slammed with layoffs. Flint has become one of America's murder capitals. In 2010, with a population of 102,000, there were 66 documented murders in Flint. The murder rate is higher than Newark, St. Louis, and New Orleans, and even Baghdad's. Flint has laid off two-thirds of its police force over the last 3 years and a typical Saturday night has experienced reduced staffing to only six patrolmen on duty (LeDuff 2011).

CAMDEN, NEW JERSEY POLICE DEPARTMENT – In January 2011 the Camden Police force was nearly cut in half. One hundred and sixty-three officers were laid off, leaving Camden with only 204 sworn officers—the department's lowest number since 1949 (Goldstein 2011).

---

1. Stratification is by agency size with all 100-plus sworn departments sampled.

- Major Cities Chiefs Association found that 52 percent of agencies surveyed had laid off sworn officers (McFarland 2010).

- According to the PERF survey, 22 percent of respondents indicated they had laid off employees as a result of decreasing budgets (PERF 2010).

COPS Hiring Program Data Indicate Number of Officers Requested to Refill Positions on the Rise

CHP applicants are eligible to apply for funds in order to a) hire new officers, b) rehire officers who had already been laid off as a result of state, local, or tribal budget cuts, and/ or c) rehire officers who are currently scheduled to be laid off on a future date as a result of budget cuts. Additionally, agencies were asked to identify which of these categories they would intend to use the hiring funds toward, if they were to receive an award.

In FY2009, 2.3 percent of applicants applied for funds to rehire at least one officer who had previously been laid off due to budget cuts. These positions made up 1.5 percent of the total number of positions requested. In comparison, in FY2011 4.6 percent of applicants applied for funds to rehire at least one officer who had previously been laid off due to budget cuts, making up 5.3 percent of the total amount of positions requested.

In FY2009, 12 percent of applicants applied for funds to rehire officers who were scheduled to be laid off. These requests made up 13 percent of the total amount of positions requested. Comparatively, in FY2011, 6 percent of applicants applied for funding to rehire officers scheduled for layoffs, making up 7.4 percent of the total positions requested.

So while the percentage of agencies requesting CHP funds in order to prevent future layoffs has decreased, the percentage of agencies requesting funds to rehire officers who have already been laid off has tripled along with the number of 'rehire positions' requests (from 1.5 percent of the total requests in 2009 to 5.3 percent of the total requests in 2011) (see Figure 6 on page 15). This indicates that many agencies had to lay off a number of officers between 2009 and 2011, and therefore are requesting funds in order to reinstate some of their sworn personnel. This is further supported by the data in which 6 percent of total applicants in FY2009 stated that they had laid off a percentage of their sworn staff, while in FY2011 this number increased to 12 percent of total applicants.

Agency Types—Request for Funds to Rehire Laid Off Officers

In 2011, a total of 125 agencies applied for positions to rehire officers. A total of 478 rehired officer positions were requested. Interestingly, the amount of rehire positions requested was fairly even when categorized by agency size (agencies serving populations of 100,000 or more were considered "large agencies"). One hundred and twelve small agencies applied to rehire a total of 233 officers. The number of positions requested within small agencies ranged from 1 to 14, with an average request of 2 officers per agency. Thirteen large agencies applied to rehire a total of 245 officers. The number of positions requested by large agencies ranged from 1 to 50, with an average request of 19 officers per agency (see Table 1 on page 15).

Table 1. Total number of agencies and rehire positions requested in 2011 by agency type

Agency Type	Number of Agencies	Number of Rehire Requests
SMALL:		
Tribal	1	1
Regional Police Department	1	3
School/Universities	5	6
Sheriff Departments	21	41
Municipal Agencies	84	182
LARGE:		
Sheriff Departments	8	148
Municipal Agencies	5	97

Source: The COPS Office

In 2011, rehiring of layoffs accounted for 14 percent of total requests by municipal agencies. By comparison, the rate for Sheriff Departments was 11 percent.

Agency Types—Request for Funds to Prevent Scheduled Layoffs
Also in 2011, a total of 172 agencies applied for at least one position in order to prevent a scheduled layoff of a sworn officer (see Table 2 on page 16). A total of 664 positions were applied for, totaling $18,207,013 in requests. One hundred and fifty-four small agencies applied for 313 preventive layoff positions. The number of positions requested ranged from 1 to 6, with an average of 2 positions per agency. Large agencies made up the majority of the requests for preventive layoff positions. Seventeen agencies applied for 351 positions, ranging from 3 to 50, with an average of 16 positions per agency.

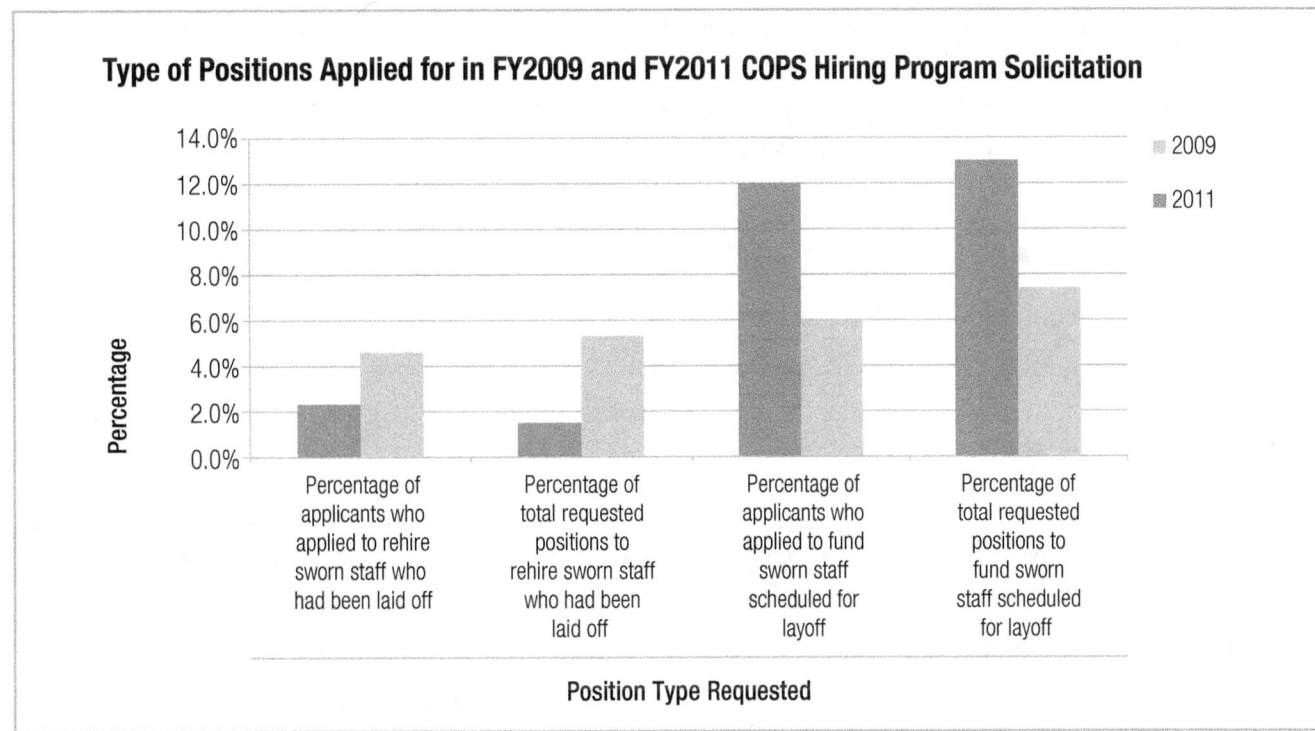

Figure 6. Comparison of types of positions requested in the COPS Hiring Program in 2009 and 2011

Source: The COPS Office

Table 2. Total number of agencies and positions in 2011 requesting funds for preventive layoff positions

Agency Type	Number of Agencies	Number of Preventative Layoff Requests
SMALL:		
Constable	1	1
County Government	1	1
Tribal	1	1
Schools	5	6
Sheriff Departments	33	64
Municipal Police	113	240
LARGE:		
Sheriff Departments	7	78
Municipal Police	10	273

Source: The COPS Office

In 2011, preventive layoff requests accounted for 25 percent of total requests by municipal agencies. By comparison the rate for Sheriff Departments was 8 percent.

Mandatory Furloughs

Many agencies are using furloughs as a method of managing labor costs. According to the PERF survey, 16 percent of responding agencies indicated they had implemented unpaid furloughs (PERF 2010). In the COPS Hiring Application, agencies were asked to report the percentage of their sworn positions that have been furloughed for at least 40 hours in the year of application. In looking at the 1,569 agencies that applied for CHP funding in both FY2009 and again in FY2011:

- In 2009 3.4 percent of these agencies reported that at least some of the sworn officers were furloughed for 40 hours or more that year.
- By 2011 the percentage reporting furloughs had more than doubled to 6.9 percent for those same agencies (see Figure 7 on page 17).

For those agencies with furloughs in either year, the percentage of staff subject to the furlough also increased dramatically from 2009 to 2011 (see Figure 8 on page 17):

- In 2009 39 percent of the officers in a furlough-affected agency were subject to the furlough.
- By 2011 57 percent of the officers in a furlough-affected agency were subject to the 40+ hour furlough.

Based on the size of our sample, it is possible to estimate that more than 28,000 officers nationwide have been furloughed for at least 40 hours this year, which is equivalent to more than 500 full-time positions.

Staffing Reductions through Attrition

As agencies are doing all they can to avoid layoffs and furloughs, many are instituting hiring freezes in order to balance operational budgets through voluntary departures.

- In the survey by National League of Cities, the most common reaction regarding personnel-related cuts made in 2010 was hiring freezes (74 percent) (McFarland 2010).

- In the 2011 National Association of Counties survey, 41 percent of responding counties stated they had instituted hiring freezes as a means of adjusting their budgets in light of revenue shortfalls (Byers 2011).

- Thirty-six percent of agencies who responded to the PERF survey stated they had experienced reduced staffing levels through attrition (PERF 2010).

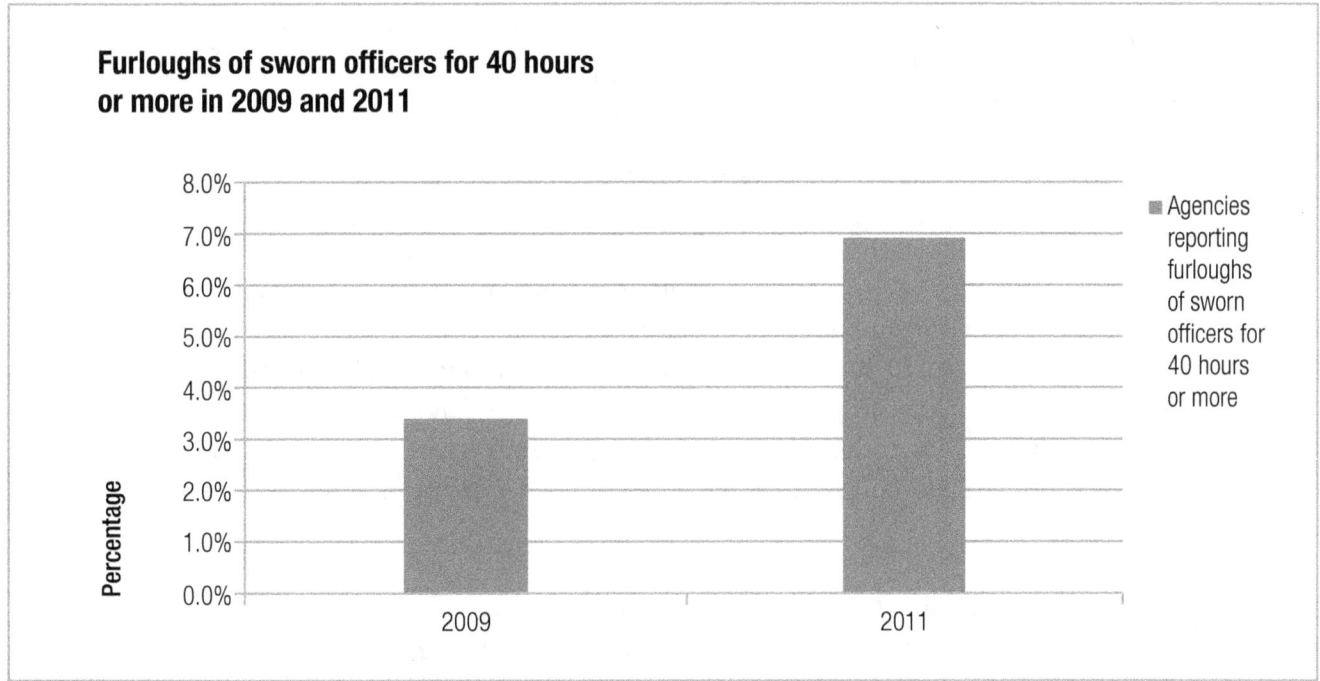

Figure 7. Comparison of agencies reporting furloughs for 40+ hours in 2009 and 2011

Source: The COPS Office

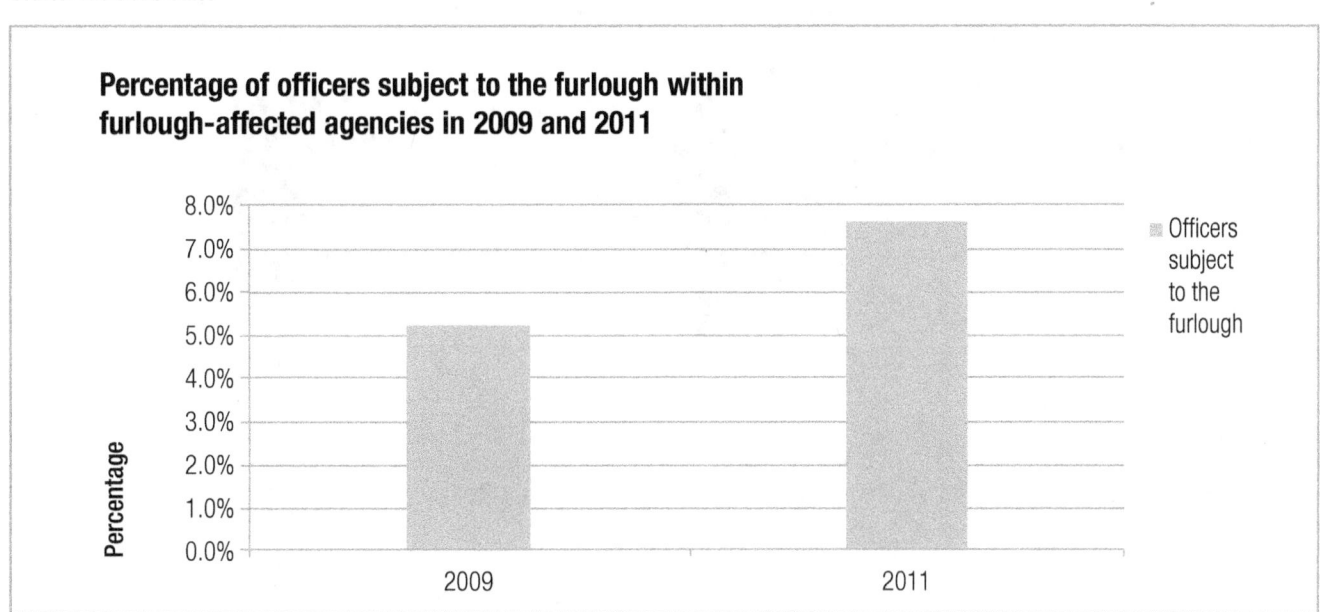

Figure 8. Comparison of the percentage of officers subject to furloughs in 2009 and 2011

Source: The COPS Office

▪ According to the 2011 CHP data, 43 percent of total applicants indicated they had sworn positions that went unfilled due to budget restraints.

Shift in Average Number of Officers per Population Served

LEMAS reports from 2004 and 2008 show the average officers per population to be about 250 per 100,000 (see Figure 9) (LEMAS 2011). This can vary dramatically across the country and between types and settings of agencies, but that number did hold steady for the 10 years prior to the recession.

In 2009, the CHP applicants had (across all agency sizes) an average of 215 officers per 100,000. In 2011, CHP applicants (across all agency sizes) had an average of only 184 officers per 100,000 (see Figure 9). Again, looking at the sample of applicants who applied in both years with more than 10 officers:

▪ In 2009 the sample agencies averaged 189 officers per 100,000
▪ By 2011 that average had dropped to 181 officers per 100,000

While this may not seem like a dramatic difference, statistical analysis revealed it to be significant, meaning that it is a greater decline than we would expect to see through random chance. In addition, the 1,569 agencies in our sample serve 4.2 million people, so the impact of even small decreases can likely be felt by many. However, this result could also be due to sample bias—meaning agencies with a lower number of officers per thousand are more likely to apply for COPS Office grant funding.

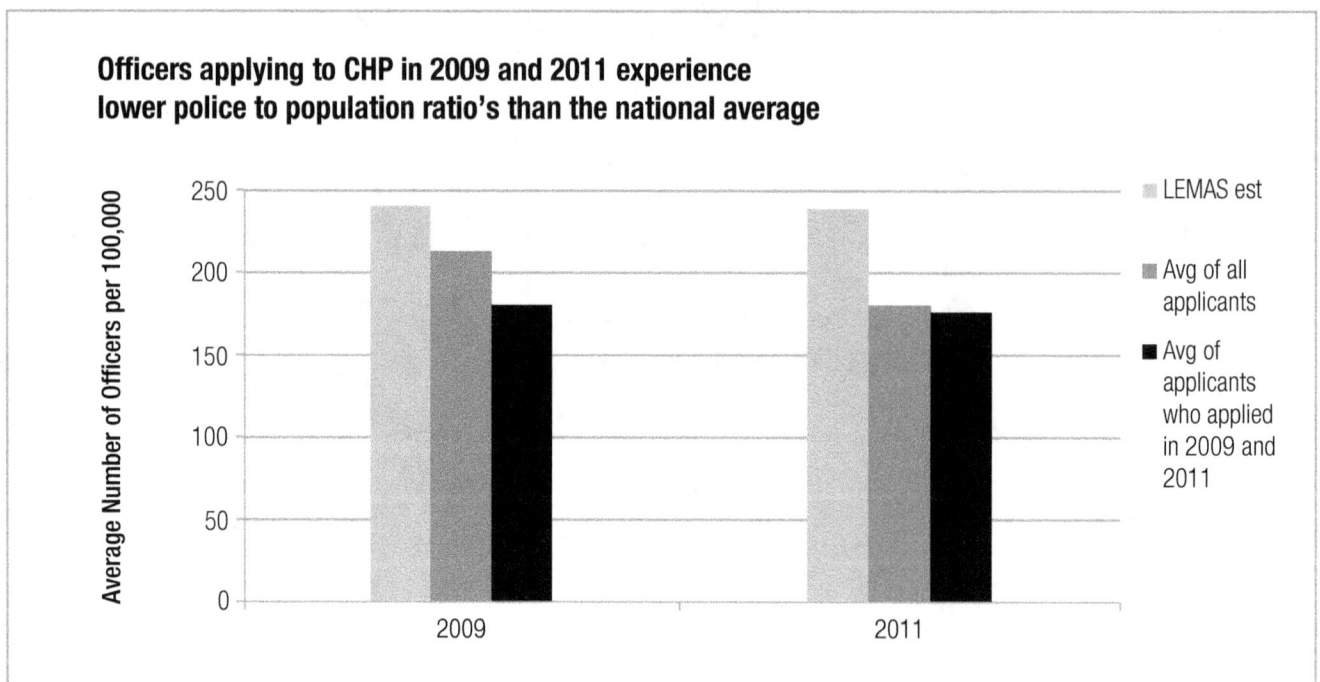

Figure 9. The average number of officers per 100,000 among CHP applicants compared to national average

Sources: Bureau of Justice Statistics and The COPS Office

COPS Hiring Program Provides Relief to Agencies Suffering from Personnel Reductions

IN THE NEWS:

BURTON, MICHIGAN – The Burton Police Department has used 2010 COPS funding to rehire two officers who were laid off as a result of budget cuts. Police Chief John Benthall said the grant "will help the Burton Police Department to maintain adequate services in the city of Burton." Budget cuts required the department to lay off two officers while losing three to attrition. In rehiring these two officers, Burton is able to "bring our police force back up to a good level," Benthall stated, and they were "ecstatic to get the news" (Acosta 2011).

FEDERAL WAY, WASHINGTON – "I'm planning to utilize this grant to maintain officers I'd otherwise have to terminate." – Police Chief Brian Wilson of Federal Way, Washington, said of the $1.03 million award the agency received in 2010 (Howard 2010).

EGG HARBOR TOWNSHIP, NEW JERSEY – Five Egg Harbor Township police officers who received layoff notices earlier in the year were able to stay on the job after the township was awarded $1.1 million through the COPS Hiring Program. "This should be a major relief to those young officers who went through the layoff ordeal in the past 2 years, serving the township the best they could while continuously worrying what will occur in 2011," Chief Blaze Catania said in a statement. "I'm very happy for them and what this means to the township and its citizens" (Rose 2010).

TULSA, OKLAHOMA – In January 2010 the Tulsa Police Department was forced to lay off 124 officers due to budget cuts. According to Tulsa Deputy Police Chief Daryl Webster, "There probably hasn't been a layoff in this department since the Depression." However, with the help of COPS funding, 18 Tulsa police officers who were laid off were re-hired. "You're talking about [reinstating] almost an entire shift of officers in one of our divisions….Certainly, it's a blessing," Webster said (Loren 2010).

BEATRICE, NEBRASKA – In 2009, the city of Beatrice received COPS funding that allowed them to retain one officer who would have otherwise been laid off. Police Chief Bruce Land said the grant will significantly impact the community. With a police force of only 22 officers—a percentage of only 1.8 officers per 1,000 residents—"To lose even one position would be a great loss," Land said (Masoner 2009).

PEORIA, ILLINOIS – The jobs of 10 Peoria police officers were saved through funds from the COPS hiring grant. The news came to the city just days after they had to make the hard decision to lay off 13 officers because of budget reductions. "This is good for the officers, this is good for the community, and this is good for the (City Council)," said Peoria Police Chief Steven Settingsgaard during a 2010 news conference. The department had lost 33 police officers the previous year in order to close a $14.5 million budget deficit. Settingsgaard stated; "The thought of seeing another significant layoff here at the Police Department has been weighing heavy on our minds. The grant could not have come at a better time and it will directly benefit the community by keeping more police officers in the streets" (Oldendorf 2010).

Effects on Delivery of Services

The effects of such staffing reductions are likely to influence the capacity of law enforcement agencies to provide the same services, in the same ways, as they have in the past. The PERF study revealed that this indeed is the case for many of their respondents. Nearly half (47 percent) of the responding agencies surveyed by PERF indicated that budget cuts had already caused or will cause changes in the services they provide to their communities. Further:

- Eight percent of departments surveyed are no longer responding to all motor vehicle thefts.
- Nine percent of departments are no longer responding to all burglar alarms.
- Fourteen percent of departments are no longer responding to all non-injury motor vehicle accidents (PERF 2010).

The MCCA survey found that 25 percent of their respondents had experienced service reductions as a result of budget cuts. Of those agencies, the following are ways in which the agencies compensated for such budget reductions:

- Seventeen percent of respondents said that their agency had stopped responding to some calls for service.
- Forty-three percent stated they had increased the use of telephone reporting, along with 30 percent who had increased the use of online reporting.
- Twenty-six percent stated there had been a reduction in investigations follow-ups, specifically related to property crimes, fugitive tracking, non-felony domestic assaults, financial crimes, computer crimes, narcotics, and traffic cases (MCCA 2011).

Changes in Policies and Procedures

Delivery of services is not the only area of law enforcement that is suffering due to budget cuts. Police policies and practices are undergoing a transformation in order to adapt to the economic changes. PERF found that two-thirds of their responding departments reported that they had reduced or discontinued training programs because of their limited budgets. More than half stated that they have cut back or even eliminated plans to obtain new technology (PERF 2010). The various ways departments responding to the survey have felt the impacts on policies can be seen in Table 3 on page 21.

Table 3. PERF study respondents indicating impacts of reduced budgets on policies

Percentage of PERF Study respondents indicating impacts of reduced budgets on policies	
Reduced out-of-town travel?	**72%**
Reduced or discontinued training?	**68%**
Considered increasing fees for police services?	**60%**
Cut back or eliminated plans to acquire technology?	**55%**
Discontinued special units (e.g., gang, traffic enforcement)?	**38%**
Implemented or considered a tax increase to avoid police service cuts?	**35%**
Discontinued take-home cars?	**31%**

Source: Police Executive Research Forum

The MCCA survey showed similar responses to questions relating to areas that had been cut as a result of budget reductions, as shown in Table 4.

Table 4. MCCA study respondents indicating impacts of budget cuts

Respondents of MCCA Study who indicated budget cuts were made in the following areas	
Travel	**61%**
Vehicles	**61%**
Training	**48%**
Aviation	**48%**
Community Policing	**39%**
Narcotics Enforcement	**35%**
School Resource Officers	**22%**
Federal Task Forces	**22%**

Source: Major Cities Chiefs Association

The IACP Survey further mirrored these trends, as shown in Table 5.

Table 5. IACP survey respondents indicating impacts of budget cuts (IACP 2011).

	Yes
Has your agency had to cut back on training?	**60%**
Has your agency had to cut back on buying or upgrading major equipment, such as vehicles in the last year?	**64%**
Has your agency cut back on buying or upgrading major technology such as In-Car Cameras or LPTs in the past year?	**58%**

Source: International Association of Chiefs of Police

Law Enforcement Service Reductions
IN THE NEWS:

CAMDEN, NEW JERSEY – "After the layoffs of 163 police officers, Camden is feeling the impact. Callers to 911 who report things like home burglaries or car break-ins are asked to file a report over the phone or at police headquarters; officers rarely respond in person. 'If it doesn't need a gun and a badge at that location,' officers are not sent, the city's police chief, J. Scott Thomson, said last week" (Goldstein 2011).

OAKLAND, CALIFORNIA – "Cutbacks…have forced police to tell residents to file their own reports—either online or in writing—for break-ins and other lesser crimes. 'If you come home to find your house burglarized and you call, we're not coming,' said Oakland Police spokeswoman Holly Joshi. The city laid off 80 officers from its force of 687 [in July] and the department can't respond to burglary, vandalism, and identity theft" (Johnson 2010a).

PERF – "For the first time, because of the economy, police departments…may have to change how they do business," says Chuck Wexler, executive director of the Police Executive Research Forum. "People will see a change in basic delivery of services," from longer police response times to a dramatically reduced police presence in some communities (Johnson 2009).

SACRAMENTO, CALIFORNIA – "The Sacramento Police Department is dealing with severe budget cuts this year, including fewer officers and task forces. A total of 43 officers lost their jobs, and the narcotics unit and gang unit was cut all together. The police department also does not respond to home burglaries unless they are in progress, and they don't respond to minor traffic accidents unless some type of crime is involved" (Maher 2011).

Civilianization

Some police agencies have also begun shifting some of the duties typically reserved for sworn staff to civilian employees as a means of cost savings. The term civilianization generally refers to a law enforcement agency's hiring of non-sworn personnel in order to replace or supplement its current sworn staff (Forst 2000). In utilizing civilians to perform duties typically performed by sworn staff, police departments are able to save money primarily through lower pay, reduced training requirements, and smaller overhead requirements. According to a study by American University Professor Brian Forst on *The Privatization and Civilization of Policing*, estimates from New York City indicate the average cost of civilian employees is about one-third to one-half that of a sworn officer, even when they are performing the same functions (Forst 2000).

More and more cities across America have begun to make the shift toward civilianization under the current budget constraints. In fact, 22 percent of respondents in the IACP survey stated their departments had begun shifting sworn responsibilities to non-sworn personnel (IACP 2011).

Police Civilianization

IN THE NEWS:

MESA, ARIZONA – The Mesa Police Department has begun using civilians for everything from crime scene processing to fraud investigations. They created a team of nine civilian investigators who make 30 to 40 percent less than an officer. In 2010, the unit handled about 50 percent of all burglary calls (Adams 2011).

OKLAHOMA CITY, OKLAHOMA – In Oklahoma City, civilians working as part-time police ambassadors help relieve some of the light duties formally performed by police, such as giving directions or working special events. For $9 an hour, these civilians provide a significant cost savings for the department. Sergeant Baxter of Oklahoma City PD has said, "They do provide what I believe is a vital service. They do help the police departments and officers out on the streets" (Loren 2010).

SAN FRANSICO, CALIFORNIA – "In San Francisco, the police department unveiled a test program last year [2010] that uses civilian investigators to respond to nonviolent crimes. They interview victims and witnesses, write reports, take crime scene photos, and collect fingerprint and DNA evidence" (Fenton 2011). "The $1 million pilot program and others like it are being designed to allow dwindling numbers of uniform officers to focus on more serious violent crime. San Francisco Assistant Chief Thomas Shawyer says the civilians will save up to $40,000 per person in training, equipment, and benefit costs required to hire an officer" (Johnson 2010b).

In BJS's report, *Census of State and Local Law Enforcement Agencies*, 2008, analysis reveals that between 1992 and 2008 the number of sworn full-time personnel in state and local law enforcement agencies grew by 34 percent, with the growth among civilian personnel (a 54.7 percent increase) outpacing growth among sworn personnel (a 25.9 percent increase). In 2008, civilian employees accounted for 32.5 percent of full-time employees in U.S. law enforcement agencies compared to 28.2 percent in 1992. Based on the 2008 BJS survey, sheriff's departments had a substantially higher proportion of civilian employees (48.2 percent) than local police departments (22.5 percent). The civilianization trend between 1992 and 2008 was much more pronounced in sheriff's departments relative to local police departments. Between 1992 and 2008, the number of civilian employees employed by sheriff's departments grew by 91 percent (relative to 34.0 percent growth in sworn employees). In contrast, the growth of civilian employees among local police was more modest at 26.7 percent (and only slightly above the 23.1 percent growth of sworn employees) (CSLLEA 2008).

Law Enforcement and Private Security Collaboration

The combination of increased demands and stagnant or declining local law enforcement resources makes it clear that, now more than ever, law enforcement agencies must pursue all reasonable avenues for collaboration with private security. Private Security is defined in the COPS publication *Operation Partnership* as, "both the proprietary (corporate) security and contract security firms across the full spectrum of security services and technology" (Law Enforcement – Private Security Consortium 2009).

At the field level, private security has the potential to reduce the cost of public law enforcement.

- In Las Vegas, Wilmington (DE), Minneapolis, New York, and other cities, law enforcement's ability to view private security closed-circuit television (CCTV) cameras has the potential to save taxpayer money that would have otherwise been spent to buy this same equipment.
- In Durham, North Carolina, and in several counties in Florida, private transit security officers are being used on public transit systems (Law Enforcement – Private Security Consortium 2009).

Data from the 2011 National Survey of County Elected Officials indicate that 23 percent of surveyed officials stated that their county has privatized one or more services once supplied by the county government due to economic conditions (McFarland 2010).

Using Volunteers

Another technique that is being used by law enforcement agencies to help manage personnel cutbacks is the use of volunteers whenever possible. In the Department of Justice National Institute of Justice report on "Strategic Cutback Management," supplementing staff with volunteers when feasible is highlighted as having significant cost saving potential (Wiseman 2011).

Using volunteers to help supplement sworn staff is a possible way for law enforcement agencies to continue to enhance the safety of the community, through increasing the efficiency of sworn personnel and promoting the partnership of citizens and police in a time when police agencies are losing manpower. The North Miami Beach Police Department Neighborhood Services and Inspections (NSI) Unit has taken volunteerism to a unique level by using police "recruits from local academies to volunteer their time to gain experience in the field." The NSI Community Policing Cadet Program allows "these cadets [to] patrol the city for quality of life issues, offering a valuable service—providing free services to the agency" (Alqadi 2011).

Agencies across the nation have begun to take part in volunteer programs after the creation of the USA Freedom Corps (USAFC) by President Bush in 2002, which resulted from the September 11, 2001 attacks. The national Volunteers in Police Service (VIPS) Program provides access to resources and information for and about law enforcement volunteer programs of all kinds and is one of five Citizen Corps partner programs that developed as part of the USAFC initiative. The program aims to improve the ability of state and local law enforcement to utilize civilian volunteers (Volunteers in Police Services 2011a). IACP manages and implements the VIPS Program in partnership with the White House Office of the USAFC and the U.S. Department of Justice Bureau of Justice Assistance.

In 2009, IACP conducted a survey of 115 law enforcement agencies that had registered VIPS Programs. The data provide a good overview of law enforcement volunteerism from the field's perspective. Of the 115 respondents, the following responses were rated according to perceived importance. The percentages below represent the number of respondents who indicated that the described factor was "important" or "very important"

- Ninety-four percent cited added value to the department
- Ninety-two percent cited the ability for officers to respond to more pressing needs
- Ninety percent cited it increased their ability to provide additional service
- Eighty-five percent cited enhancing citizens understanding of the police (Volunteers in Policing Services 2011b)

IACP has also found a vast increase in the number of volunteers that are being used by law enforcement agencies to perform police duties since 2004 (see Figure 10) (Johnson 2010b).

Furthermore, 43 percent of MCCA survey respondents reported that they increased the use of volunteers as a means to compensate for budget reductions (MCCA 2011).

DUE TO COPYRIGHT RESTRICTIONS
SOME OR ALL IMAGES ARE NOT INCLUDED

Figure 10. Data provided by IACP on the number of citizen volunteers used by police agencies from 2004 to 2010

* Data are through 10/6/2010

Source: International Association of Chiefs of Police

Law Enforcement Agency's Use of Volunteers
IN THE NEWS:

RICHLAND, WASHINGTON – "In Richland a group of nearly 40 volunteers is taking on the smaller tasks, lightening the workload so cops can stay focused on more serious threats—all for free.... Richland's Police Volunteers logged more than 600 hours just last month, providing that sense of security to more and more people" (Vedadi 2011).

DURHAM, NORTH CAROLINA – "Teams of civilian volunteers help police canvass neighborhoods immediately after murders and other violent crimes, to help responding units and put potential witnesses at ease. Durham Chief Jose Lopez says other volunteers in city-issued cars patrol shopping centers during the busy holiday seasons and conduct property checks for residents who are away from home. 'They are additional eyes and ears for us,' Lopez says. 'It effectively puts more people on the street'" (Johnson 2010b).

WACO, TEXAS – "Students from Baylor College, Texas State Technical College, and McClennan Community College can earn college credit in political science while learning about the law enforcement profession first-hand. Citizens on Patrol student volunteers help patrol the Baylor campus and direct traffic during special events. The patrol is especially active during Christmas break and other school holidays, when fewer 'eyes and ears' are typically around to report crimes" (USAonWatch n.d.).

LOS ANGELES, CALIFORNIA – Due to a $100 million cut in budget, LAPD will use volunteers to fill the gap. Currently there are 700 unpaid workers in its Reserve Corps—saving the city about $5 million each year (Hillard 2011).

Technology as a Force Multiplier

Around the country, cash-strapped communities are looking for any way to boost efficiency and cut spending. As indicated in several of the current surveys, many law enforcement agencies have been forced to reduce or entirely cut their budgets for technology (more than half of the PERF study respondents stated they had cut back or eliminated plans to acquire technology) (PERF 2010). However, other police agencies are shifting their operational models to include the use of technology systems that can help agencies to improve outcomes and increase efficiency. Certain technologies such as Closed-Circuit Televisions (CCTVs) and Light-Based Intervention Systems (LBIS) can act as force multipliers through incident intervention and crime prevention, without requiring the immediate presence of an officer (Cordero 2011).

A recent COPS publication, *Evaluating the Use of Public Surveillance Cameras for Crime Control and Prevention*, studied the public surveillance systems in Baltimore, MD, Chicago, IL, and Washington, D.C. A cost-benefit analysis was used to analyze the cost of the surveillance systems with the savings from victim and criminal justice costs. One neighborhood in Chicago alone saw a cost savings of $4.30 for every dollar that was used for the system. Most law enforcement agencies have to balance the cost of implementing, maintaining, and training for a new piece of technology with the savings that this technology will bring, and this study provides some interesting examples (La Vigne et al. 2011).

Some agencies have increased the use of a type of geographical technology called the Tactical Automatic Vehicle Locator (TAC-AVL) which is used to reduce police response times to emergency calls. TAC-AVL provides commanders the locations of patrols cars with a real-time map of the city, allowing them to determine whether the vehicles are in the right place at the right time (Mayer 2009). Efficient management of resources is crucial for agencies with limited manpower. Automated Emergency Dispatch Systems (AEDs) are used in some agencies to automate emergency police dispatch by electronically locating and dispatching the nearest available patrols (Cordero 2011).

A new trend developing in law enforcement agencies today is the use of social media. According to a PERF survey, 86 percent of responding agencies used some form of social media, including Facebook, Twitter, MySpace, YouTube, and Nixle. Social media provides a cost effective avenue for police to communicate directly with their communities, as well as receive information and feedback from those that they serve (Johnson 2011).

Police Use of Technology as Force Multiplier

IN THE NEWS:

ALBUQUERQUE, NEW MEXICO – Albuquerque police have led the way in utilizing technology and social media to make up for the loss of officers and resources due to budget cuts. Their system provides "real-time investigative information to private business groups on interactive websites to help stop theft rings, locate violent crime suspects, and track fugitives. Police Chief Raymond Schultz has said that the system has helped make up for the loss of about 60 officers over the past 2 ½ years. The Albuquerque model is now being replicated in agencies in Georgia, Minnesota, Washington, and California" (Johnson 2011).

CAMDEN, NEW JERSEY – Camden Police use a combination of GPS, gunshot detectors, and CCTVs to identify problem areas and dispatch officers to those places, which is more efficient than waiting for calls for service. "Technology can never fully replace an officer," said Camden Police Chief Scott Thomson, whose department of 250 officers has been nearly cut in half since 2006. "We are just trying to leverage technology...to appear bigger than we are" (Johnson 2011).

FULTON COUNTY, GEORGIA – "Fulton County has received permission from the Board of Supervisors' Public Safety Committee to accept a one-time state grant of $30,000 for teleconferencing equipment.... The Sheriff's Department currently spends about 6 hours a day [at the courthouse]; 'The video teleconferencing will help reduce transportation costs' by allowing computerized court appearances" (Anich 2011).

BELMONT COUNTY, OHIO – "A juvenile court in eastern Ohio has found that instituting video court hearings has decreased costs and increased the delivery of swift services. Juvenile Court Judge Mark Costine who began the program has found that by reducing the number of prisoner transports, the sheriff's office has saved $50,000 year, while the video installation only cost about $7,000. Judge Costine notes; 'All the courts have these issues of transportation of prisoners....We have found a way to make the hearings go faster and also save money'" (Long 2011).

The Boca Raton (Florida) Police Department has created a social media project called VIPER (Visibility, Intelligence, Partnerships, Education, and Resources), which provides the community with a forum to share crime tips, view recent mug shots, receive information, or even request emergency services (Madeiros 2011).

Chuck Wexler, the executive director of PERF, has said; "Departments are looking to technology as a force multiplier. They are using this technology to better manage fewer resources, because just saying 'We don't have enough officers' isn't cutting it with the public" (Johnson 2011).

Another example of how technology has been leveraged by police agencies forced to reduce spending, is through the use of video teleconferencing. For judicial proceedings that had previously required inmates to appear in court, and therefore required an official to transport them, videoconferencing provides some agencies with an efficient and resourceful tool to provide services at a reduced cost. Through the use of teleconferencing equipment, court proceedings are able to be held via video as lawyers discuss their cases in front of the judge, instead of having a constable, sheriff, or police officer transport the defendants to court.

A survey conducted by the Administrative Office of Pennsylvania Courts' (AOPC) Office of Judicial Security, on the use of video conferencing as a means of conducting preliminary arraignments and other judicial proceedings, found that utilization of this technology had a cost savings potential of $21 million annually. Results from the study showed that on average, more than 15,700 proceedings are currently being held via video conferencing in Pennsylvania, resulting in a cost savings of about $1.7 million monthly (AOPC 2011).

Eliminating court transports has the potential to save agencies both monetarily and through officer productivity. A typical prisoner transport involves one officer and one car for what can take up to an entire day. The AOPC study found on average it costs $73 to transport a defendant to and from a local facility and an addition $588 to transport to and from a state correctional institution (AOPC 2011). The cost savings realized as a result of implementing this new method of service delivery have been staggering in some places, including annual savings of $30 million in Pennsylvania, $600,000 in Georgia, and $50,000 in Ohio from transportation costs alone (Long 2011).

Effects on Organizational Management

With agencies nationwide struggling to uphold their levels of service while losing personnel, many have been forced to consolidate efforts with neighboring agencies. The term *consolidation*, as used here, describes a number of concepts related to the pooling of resources between law enforcement agencies. In 2007, the New Jersey State Association of Chiefs of Police published the white paper *Police Department Regionalization, Consolidation, Merger & Shared Services: Important Considerations for Policy Makers*, and defined the different types of consolidation efforts as follows:

Shared Services: Is when two or more agencies combine certain function units, such as emergency communications, SWAT, dispatch, or records.

Local Merger/Consolidation: When two separate police agencies form a single new unit.

Regionalization: When a number of jurisdictions combine efforts to police a geographic area rather than a jurisdictional one. The new entity does not contain elements of any existing agency—either the jurisdictions had no previously-existing police department, or those that existed have been disbanded.

Contract Services: Is when a formal contract to pay for law enforcement services is provided by one jurisdiction to one or more other jurisdictions (NJSACOP 2007: 2).

State and local law enforcement agencies throughout the country are finding the need to develop effective methods and strategies in order to compensate for their dwindling resources. In order to keep communities safe in an affordable and cost effective way, some police agencies are combining their efforts to optimize productivity and increase efficiency (Cordero 2011).

Studies of Law Enforcement Agency Consolidation

- In the 2011 National Survey of County Elected Officials, 26 percent of respondents said that their county had consolidated services with another county government in response to economic conditions. Further, another 31 percent said that their county has participated in discussions regarding the consolidation of services (McFarland 2010).

- One quarter of IACP survey respondents referenced innovative multi-jurisdictional arrangements their department was taking to promote cost-effective service delivery, including:
    - Joint task forces, combinations that include police, sheriffs, state police, and constables.
    - Service/function-specific resource sharing, including crime scene technicians, dispatch, SWAT, Hazmat, laboratories, and training (IACP 2011).

- Seventy-seven percent of IACP survey respondents said that their agency has been asked to increase its support of other agencies (IACP 2011).

- Seventy percent of MCCA survey respondents stated that they had used consolidation of functions as a means to compensate for budget reductions (MCCA 2011).

- In the 2011 National Association of Counties survey, 38 percent of respondents said that they had been approached by other units of the government during FY2010 about consolidating various activities. Of those approached, 23 percent said they have consolidated law enforcement and/or fire protection (Byers 2011).

- In the 2011 National Survey of County Elected Officials, 56 percent of respondents indicated that their county had cooperated regionally to reduce the cost of services (McFarland 2010).

- A study conducted by Cumberland County, New Jersey, found that the cities could collectively save $4.5 million over 5 years through consolidation (Zager 2011).
- Somerville, New Jersey, also conducted a study, which found that regionalizing their municipal police services under one county umbrella could save about $18 million a year (Cooper 2011).

Regionalization and Consolidation
IN THE NEWS:

MINNEAPOLIS/SAINT PAUL, MINNESOTA – In the Twin Cities of Minneapolis/Saint Paul, the Police Authority and the San Anselmo Police Department began taking steps towards consolidation by sharing some dispatch services and officers. The proposed plan would save San Anselmo $51,000 immediately, and another $113,000 in the future (Dunleavy 2011).

PORTAGE, MICHIGAN – Portage has consolidated the police and fire departments. The city's police chief has taken the role of public safety director, reporting directly to the deputy city manager, and is responsible for the overall management of both the fire and police departments (Hall 2011).

NEW JERSEY – Berlin Township, Berlin Borough, and Waterford Township Police Departments in New Jersey have developed their own approach to sharing public safety services by combining their police detectives in a shared investigative bureau. Further, Berlin's volunteer fire department is being used to staff evening hour shifts in order to save costs (Mast 2011).

CAMDEN COUNTY, NEW JERSEY – Camden County is developing alternate plans for regionalized special services, such as a central detective bureau and SWAT (SNJDC 2011).

MARION COUNTY, OREGON – "Marion County Board of County Commissioners (Fire Rescue/Public Safety Communications) and the Marion County Sheriff's Office are initiating efforts to combine their dispatch services. County and Sheriff's Office staff determined that consolidating those efforts would create a recurring savings of $370,000 per year" (Bryant 2011).

LANSING, MICHIGAN – "A plan to consolidate Lansing's north and south police precincts could save the city $535,380 in rent, utilities, and janitorial services by the 2015 fiscal year" (VanHulle 2011).

GREENFIELD, CALIFORNIA – The Greenfield City Council approved an agreement to merge its police force with the city of Soledad's. City Manager Brent Slama stated, "'Given the fiscal realities facing our cities, especially the four south Monterey County cities, regionalization is going to be important [in the future].' The Soledad proposal is projected to save Greenfield $158,699 beginning in the 2012–13 fiscal year. David Cariaga [a representative of both Greenfield Police associations] stated, 'It's the best solution to keep the men and women in the department working and…it's creating a savings for the city'" (Vijayan 2011).

BROWARD COUNTY, FLORIDA – "Facing an estimated $9 million deficit, mostly for police and fire services, Lauderdale Lakes has asked the Sheriff's Office for help. The solution came in the form of consolidation between Lauderdale Lakes and the unincorporated Central Broward district, which will save a combined $3.4 million. 'Many of our cities ought to look to merge with each other and have economies of scale and save the taxpayers a lot of money,' Broward County Commissioner Dale Holness said at a June County Commission workshop" (East 2011).

The Importance of Community Policing in Tough Financial Times

Many of the cost saving techniques discussed within this report are directly related to community policing efforts. Community policing is a philosophy that promotes organizational strategies, which support the systematic use of partnerships and problem-solving techniques, to proactively address the immediate conditions that give rise to public safety issues such as crime, social disorder, and fear of crime (COPS Office 2009a). The three tenets of community policing—community partnerships, organizational transformation, and problem solving—are of increased importance when facing budget cuts that reduce the number of officers on the streets.

Collaborative partnerships to develop solutions to problems and increase trust in police can be seen in many of the solutions police agencies are using in light of the economic downturn. Specifically, the use of volunteers, partnerships between the police and private agencies, and the use of social media as a means to communicate effectively with the community in order to meet their needs, are all examples of how collaborative partnerships act as a cost-saving tool.

Organizational transformation exists through the alignment of organizational management, structure, personnel, and information systems to support community partnerships and proactive problem solving. From its inception, community policing's goal is one of forging strong relationships between law enforcement and the communities they serve. It aims to redesign the practice of public safety into a collective, collaborative effort (COPS Office 2009a).

The current economic crisis, which has thwarted many police activities, requires police agencies to place a greater emphasis on problem-solving techniques. By engaging in the proactive and systematic examination of identified problems and developing and rigorously evaluating effective responses, they will be able to best use the limited resources that are available to them.

Unfortunately, when agencies are forced to make widespread budget cuts, some have done so by reducing or eliminating some of their community policing programs. In fact, according to the MCCA survey, 39 percent of respondents who have reduced budgets stated that those budgets cuts were made to their community policing efforts (MCCA 2011).

Herein lies one of the major fallacies as it relates to community policing. Community policing should not be viewed as a particular program within a department, but rather as a department-wide philosophy. Programs are typically initiated as a response to a specific problem, in which only a small portion of the organization is involved and once the problem has been addressed the program is dissolved (Trojanowicz and Bucqueroux 1994). Instead, community policing must be understood as a philosophy that promotes the systematic use of partnerships and problem-solving techniques to proactively address the conditions within a community that are cause for public concerns over crime and social disorder issues (Melekian 2011d).

Community policing is an organizational strategy. It can be used to govern the way police services are delivered, recognizing the police officer as an organizer of resources in pursuit of public safety rather than someone designated to perform specific tasks (Trojanowicz and Bucqueroux 1994).

In an article in *The Police Chief*, COPS Office Director Melekian articulates the importance of the community policing philosophy in the face of the current economic climate. He argues that the downturn in the economy has affected the country in ways that could not have been predicted even 5 years ago. The enhancement of community policing and the myriad of social outreach programs that have been employed by local law enforcement were initially brought about in large measure by the combination of federal grant dollars and readily available local funding sources. That financial foundation is now in serious jeopardy in many local jurisdictions.

Melekian further highlights how some have made the argument that these economic challenges may compel us to abandon community policing because we simply cannot afford it (Melekian 2011d). However, experience has shown that community policing is a more cost-effective way of utilizing available resources than simple traditional policing practices, for a number of reasons. Primarily, community participation in crime-prevention amplifies the amount of available resources, while community partnerships used to address problem solving provides a more efficient distribution of combined police and community resources than simply reactive policing program models (Brown 1989).

The Importance of Community Policing in a Recession

IN THE NEWS!

CONCORD, MASSACHUSETTS – Deputy Police Chief Barry Neal has utilized the proactive approach of community policing to prevent crime and reduce victimization. "We recognize that we can't solve problems alone, we need to engage the community and work in partnership with them," he said. "It gives us direct daily face-to-face contact between the community and the officers, and also gives us the ability to prevent problems from occurring instead of reacting to them" (Ball 2009).

ALBUQUERQUE, NEW MEXICO – Chief Schultz of Albuquerque is having officers develop partnerships with retailers to address shoplifters and boosters. The Police Department has experienced a 20 percent reduction in their workforce and is developing partnerships with retailers with the goal of sharing information in order to link petty crimes together to prosecute larger and stronger cases and get repeat offenders off the street. In addition, they are offering rewards to housekeepers at hotels to report the accumulation of large amounts of merchandise, which can often be found in hotel rooms (Stelter 2011).

KANSAS CITY, MISSOURI – "When we talk in Kansas City about 'doing something different,' a mention of community policing usually follows. And surely, the thought of police officers working hand in hand with neighborhood folks is enticing. But successful, citywide community policing would require a culture change for a police department that places more faith in arrest statistics than relationships as a crime-fighting tool. [In looking for a new police chief, Kansas City] believes a chief who finds a way to make it acceptable, indeed desirable, for officers to connect with citizens and help solve problems will be the start of the change that everyone talks about" (Shelly 2011).

Conclusion

In 2008, the entire country was introduced to the largest fiscal crisis since the Great Depression. Many who have worked in the field for decades have never seen an economic situation that has affected law enforcement like the one our country currently faces. As cities and counties across America are experiencing a downturn in local revenues, the effects on public safety budgets have been significant. Americans are faced with a new economic reality, in which they are challenged to develop new and innovative ways to leverage resources and maximize productivity in the face of diminishing financial means. Police agencies have not escaped the effects of shrinking revenues. In fact, the economic challenges facing many Americans are amplified when it comes to public safety.

To compensate for shrinking budgets, many individuals focus on what can be sacrificed from their normal lifestyle in order to offset the reduction in available spending. Families may forego their annual summer vacation, or choose to only shop in discount stores rather than their favorite department stores. However, law enforcement agencies face the more difficult and ever important task of maintaining the same quality of service that they always have provided despite a severe reduction in available resources. Therefore, to successfully deliver the high levels of community protection and emergency responsiveness communities depend on, law enforcement agencies must develop new and innovative techniques to address the needs of their communities in cost-effective and sustainable ways.

The recognition and acceptance of this new economic reality is more important than ever in developing strategic management practices to ensure the effective and efficient delivery of police services. Never before has the law enforcement community experienced such significant cuts to operating budgets and available resources. Rather than continuing to provide services through traditional means in hopes that the economy will return to pre-recession levels, police nationwide are shifting, adapting, and redeveloping the ways in which they do their job—to ensure the highest levels of public safety.

In every corner of the United States, state, local, and tribal police departments are being forced to lay off officers and civilian staff, or modify their operations as a result of budget cuts. Over the last 2 years, many agencies have experienced considerable affects from budget constrictions, including mandatory furloughs and hiring freezes, which have resulted in significant reductions in staffing levels never experienced before. Indeed, American law enforcement is changing, and the effects are likely to last over the next 5 to 10 years, if not longer.

While the exact nature of how these changes will take place is unclear, the data within this report suggest that changes may occur on several fronts. First, there may be greater application of "force-multiplier" technologies such as closed-circuit TVs, automated emergency dispatch systems, video teleconferencing equipment, and social media usage. Utilization of technologies such as these has the ability to provide law enforcement agencies with a way to maximize available information while alleviating the need for an immediate response.

Another fundamental alteration that has been seen in delivery of police services as a result of the changing economy is the increased application of non-sworn individuals— both as employees and as volunteers. More and more police agencies have begun to shift some of the responsibilities that have traditionally been performed by sworn staff to civilian personnel as a means to mitigate payroll costs and maintain staffing levels. Further, some agencies have even engaged citizen volunteers to help alleviate the strain on police work loads. Such approaches can provide sworn staff with more time to focus on pressing and time-sensitive issues that can only be successfully managed by a law enforcement officer.

Some agencies have had to drastically change their methods for handling non-emergency situations and administrative duties. Many police agencies are no longer able to dispatch an officer to every call for service. Instead, more often police managers are forced to direct their resources to focus on situations which pose the most threat to public safety. For example, some agencies are no longer able send officers to collect crime reports for cases that don't involve suspects, or dispatch patrol officers to every non-emergency/non-injury service call. The primary focus on law enforcement is protecting the safety of their communities. Therefore, agencies experiencing limited resources must adjust their approach to focus in on situations that are an immediate threat to public safety.

A more drastic change that is being seen as a result of the economic downturn is the increase in the number of agencies combining efforts and resources through consolidation, shared services, and regionalization. When agencies are faced with maintaining services levels with less and less, collaborating or combining agency's efforts often is the only way to maximize available resources, training, and information.

As this report has shown, the recent economic downturn has placed serious constraints on police budgets and severely diminished the availability of resources. As an additional step to help compensate for declining resources, many departments have also begun collecting and disseminating crime data in real-time via new technology. This has allowed for the effective management and strategic deployment of resources to focus on specific problems as they develop. With the increased use of technology and information-sharing policies being institutionalized throughout many police departments nationwide, it has become essential that the collection of national census data relating to law enforcement agencies be collected with the same urgency.

It is crucial for policy makers to create proactive, aggressive, and productive problem-solving strategies based on relevant and current data. However, the delay in the current methods of data collection and dissemination makes it difficult to present an accurate picture of the state of police agencies as things happen. In turn, a true understanding of the challenges confronting law enforcement agencies as seen through comprehensive analysis takes time and resources. It will be important for federal partners to collaborate on a way to collectively participate in data collection efforts in the future that will increase the availability of up-to-date data, and its analysis and dissemination. By collecting data more frequently and comprehensively, policy makers and government agencies will be able to adjust and realign their strategic goals to provide relevant assistance where law enforcement agencies need it most.

Institutionalization of the community policing philosophy is vital to the ability of law enforcement agencies to succeed and thrive in the current economic climate. Agencies must systematically use partnerships and problem-solving techniques to proactively address the problems that their communities are facing. Development and enhancement of symbiotic relationships between police and the communities they serve is key to ensuring community safety.

It is clear that the challenges facing America as a result of the economic decline that began in 2008 have been significant. Law enforcement communities are facing a new reality in American policing—one that requires a shift in the methods they use to uphold levels of service while dealing with ever shrinking budgets. However, the importance of maintaining and expanding community policing practices during this time of economic hardship is paramount. Research and feedback from the field indicate that community policing is a successful practice in both small and large agencies with significant public safety problems. Thankfully, many of the law enforcement agencies in the United States already practice community policing, and more are coming to recognize the value of community partnerships in this time of limited resources.

References

Acosta, Roberto. 2011. "Burton officials to rehire two laid-off police officers with reworded COPS grant." *Flint Journal* July 18. www.mlive.com/news/flint/index.ssf/2011/07/burton_officials_to_bring_back.html.

Adams, Paul. 2011. "Arizona police force turns to civilian investigators." *BBC News* April 5. www.bbc.co.uk/news/world-us-canada-12754776.

Alqadi, Nazmia. 2011. Building Relationships and Solving Problems in North Miami. *Community Policing Dispatch* vol. 4, no. 10. www.cops.usdoj.gov/html/ dispatch/10-2011/North-Miami-Beach.asp.

Anich, Michael. 2011. "County eyes jail teleconferencing." *The Leader Herald* July 26. www.leaderherald.com/page/content.detail/id/539221.html.

AOPC (Administrative Office of Pennsylvania Courts). 2011. "PA Courts Expand Use of Video Conferencing, Saving $21 Million Annually in Defendant Transportation Costs." AOPC press release June 7. www.aopc.org/NR/rdonlyres/36906F45-C993-4844-A3E1-CC3A68B4300B/0/ VideoConfExpdsPACts_060711.pdf.

Ball, Patrick. 2009. "Police face budget cuts: Town could scale back Community Policing." *GateHouse News Service* May 21. www.wickedlocal.com/concord/ news/x124592912/Police-face-budget-cut-Town-could-scale-back-Community-Policing#axzz1XykF7BhL.

Brown, Lee. 1989. *Community Policing: A Practical Guide for Police Officials.* Washington, D.C.: U.S. Department of Justice, Office of Justice Programs, National Institute of Justice, NCJ118001.

Bryant, Kathy. 2011. "Dispatch consolidation a win-win for public." *Ocala.com* September 4. www.ocala.com/article/20110904/OPINION/110909913/1162/sitemaps.

Byers, Jacqueline. 2011. *The Recession Continues: An Economic Status Survey of Counties.* Washington, D.C.: National Association of Counties.

CBS Broadcasting, Inc. 2010. "Fears Rise as Patterson, N.J. Police Force Lays Off 125 Officers." *CBS Broadcasting, Inc.* April 18. http://newyork.cbslocal.com/2011/04/18/paterson-new-jersey-cuts-125-police-officers/.

Clark, Richard. 2011. *Looking for the Light at the End of the Tunnel: a national survey of county elected officials on the economy, budgets and politics.* Athens, Georgia: Carl Vinson Institute of Government.

Cooper, Warren. 2011. "Somerset County Prosecutor to update public on countywide policing effort." *Somerset Messenger-Gazette* June 2. www.nj.com/messenger-gazette/index.ssf/2011/06/somerset_county_prosecutor_to_ update_public_on_countywide_policing_effort.html.

COPS Office (Office of Community Oriented Policing Services). 2009a. *Community Policing Defined.* Washington, D.C.: U.S. Department of Justice, Office of Community Oriented Policing Services.

COPS Office (Office of Community Oriented Policing Services). 2009b. *Operation Partnership: Trends and Practices in Law Enforcement and Private Security Collaborations.* Washington, D.C.: U.S. Department of Justice, Office of Community Oriented Policing Services.

Cordero, Joe. 2011. *Reducing the Cost of Quality of Policing: Making Community Safety Cost Effective and Sustainable,* NJLM Educational Foundation, Friends of Local Government Services, vol. 3, no. 1. Trenton, New Jersey: The Cordero Group.

CSLLEA (Census of State and Local Law Enforcement Agencies), Bureau of Justice Statistics, Office of Justice Programs, U.S. Department of Justice. http://bjs.ojp.usdoj.gov/index.cfm?ty=dcdetail&iid=249.

Dunleavy, Kelly. 2011. "San Anselmo, Twin Cities Move Closer to Police Consolidation." *Patch* June 14. http://sananselmofairfax.patch.com/articles/san-anselmo-twin-cities-move-closer-to-police-consolidation.

Fenton, John. 2011. "Police reports will be taken over phone in city pilot program." *The Baltimore Sun* August 16. http://articles.baltimoresun.com/2011-08-16/news/bs-md-ci-police-report-pilot-20110816_1_crimes-largest-police-district-northeast-baltimore.

Forst, Brian. 2000. "The Privatization and Civilization of Policing." In C. M. Friel (Ed.), *Boundary Changes in Criminal Justice Organizations: Criminal Justice 2000,* Vol. 2:19–79. Washington, D.C.: National Institute of Justice. NCJ 182409.

Friend, Zack, and Rick Martinez. 2010. "Preserving Community-Oriented Policing in a Recession." *ICMA Press* April. http://webapps.icma.org/pm/9203/public/pmplus1.cfm?author=Zach%20Friend%20and%20Rick%20Martinez&title=Preserving%20Community-Oriented%20Policing%20in%20a%20Recession&subtitle.

Goldstein, Joseph. 2011. "Police Force Nearly Halved, Camden Feels Impact." *The New York Times* March 6. www.nytimes.com/2011/03/07/nyregion/07camden.html?pagewanted=all.

Hall, Rex. 2011. "Portage police and fire administration to be consolidated under one public safety director." *Kalamazoo Gazette* May 13. www.mlive.com/news/kalamazoo/index.ssf/2011/05/portage_police_and_fire_admini.html.

Henry, Samantha. 2011. "Cops protest as Paterson lays off 125 police officers; mayor hopes to hire some back." Associated Press April 18. www.guardianangels.org/pdf/99226.pdf.

Hillard, Gloria. 2011. "In Tight Times, L.A. Forced to Rely on Volunteer Police." *NPR* May 19. www.npr.org/2011/05/19/136436405/in-tight-times-l-a-relies-on-volunteer-police.

Hoene, Christopher, and Michael Pagano. 2010. *City Fiscal Conditions in 2010.* Washington, D.C.: National League of Cities.

Howard, Jacinda. 2010. "Grant will save four police jobs in Federal Way." *Federal Way Mirror* October 5. www.pnwlocalnews.com/south_king/fwm/news/104379438.html.

IACP (International Association of Chiefs of Police). 2010. *Policing in the 21st Century: Preliminary Survey Results.* Alexandria, Virginia: International Association of Chiefs of Police.

Johnson, Kevin. 2009. "Economy limiting services of local police." *USA Today* May 18. www.usatoday.com/news/nation/2009-05-17-police-closure_N.htm.

Johnson, Kevin. 2010a. "Cutbacks force police to curtail calls for some crimes." *USA Today* August 25.
www.usatoday.com/news/nation/2010-08-25-1Anresponsecops25_ST_N.htm.

Johnson, Kevin. 2010b. "Tight budgets lead to more civilians used for policing." *USA Today* October 11.
www.usatoday.com/news/nation/2010-10-11-1Acitizenpolice11_ST_N.htm.

Johnson, Kevin. 2011. "Police tap technology to compensate for fewer officers." *USA Today* April 25.
www.usatoday.com/news/nation/2011-04-24-police-crime-technology-facebook.htm.

La Vigne, Nancy, Samantha S. Lowry, Joshua A. Markman, and Allison M. Dwyer. 2011. *Evaluating the Use of Public Surveillance Cameras for Crime Control and Prevention.* Washington, D.C.: U.S. Department of Justice, Office of Community Oriented Policing Services.

LEMAS (Law Enforcement Management and Administrative Statistics), Bureau of Justice Statistics, Office of Justice Programs, U.S. Department of Justice.
http://bjs.ojp.usdoj.gov/index.cfm?ty=dcdetail&iid=248\.

LeDuff, Charlie. 2011. "Riding Along With the Cops in Murdertown, U.S.A." *The New York Times* April 15. www.nytimes.com/2011/04/17/magazine/mag-17YouRhere-t.html.

Long, Colleen. 2011. "Courts nationwide hold hearings with video." *Associated Press* May 8. http://newyork.cbslocal.com/2011/05/08/courts-nationwide-hold-hearings-with-video/.

Loren, Jennifer. 2010. "Stimulus Money Used to Save Police Jobs." *WorldNow and KWTV* February 3.
www.news9.com/story/11930579/stimulus-money-used-to-save-police-jobs.

Madeiros, James. 2011. "Police Use Social Media to Shape Image, Fight Crime." *Criminal Justice Degree Schools* June 12. www.criminaljusticedegreeschools.com/police-use-social-media-to-fight-crime-0612111/.

Maher, Jeff. 2011. "Sacramento Police handcuffed by budget cuts." *News 10/KXTV* August 29. www.news10.net/news/article/152169/2/Sacramento-police-handcuffed-by-budget-cuts-.

Masoner, Gloria. 2009. "COPS grant saves loss of Beatrice officer." *Beatrice Daily Sun* July 30. www.beatricedailysun.com/news/local/article_b452b12c-e05c-5a37-843d-01c9bf047d4c.html.

Mast, George. 2011. "When merged police forces worked in Camden County – and when they didn't." *Courier Post* June 20. http://pqasb.pqarchiver.com/courierpostonline/access/2379431651.html?FMT=ABS&date=Jun+20%2C+2011.

MCCA (Major Cities Chiefs Association). 2011. *Police Economic Challenges Survey Results.* Sun Valley, Idaho: Major Cities Chiefs Association (unpublished).

McFarland, Christina. 2010. *State of America's Cities Survey on Jobs and the Economy.* Washington, D.C.: National League of Cities, Center for Research and Innovation.

Melekian, Bernard. 2011a. Director's Message. *Community Policing Dispatch* vol. 4, no. 3. http://cops.usdoj.gov/html/dispatch/03-2011/DirectorMessage.asp.

Melekian, Bernard. 2011b. Director's Column: July 2011. *Community Policing Dispatch* vol. 4, no. 7. http://cops.usdoj.gov/html/dispatch/07-2011/DirectorMessage.asp.

Melekian, Bernard. 2011c. Director's Column: June 2011. *Community Policing Dispatch* vol. 4, no. 6. http://cops.usdoj.gov/html/dispatch/06-2011/DirectorMessage.asp.

Melekian, Bernard. 2011d. "The Office of Community Oriented Policing Services, From the Director." *The Police Chief* 78 (March): 14. www.policechiefmagazine.org/magazine/index.cfm?fuseaction=print_display&article_id=2330&issue_id=32011.

Merkle, Dan. 2011. "Data Driven Decision Making: Reducing Operating Costs While Maintaining Mission Excellence." (Presentation at the 2011 COPS Conference, Washington, D.C., August 1, 2011).

Myer, Allison. 2009. "Geospatial Technology Helps East Orange Crack Down on Crime." *Geography & Public Safety* 1, no. 4 (January):8–9.

NJSACOP (New Jersey State Association of Chiefs of Police). 2007. *Police Department Regionalization, Consolidation, Merger & Shared Services: Important Considerations for Police Makers*: 2. A NAJSACOP White Paper, West Trenton, New Jersey. www.nj.gov/dca/affiliates/luarcc/resources/pdf/WhitePaper-Consolidation.pdf.

Oldendorf, Patrick. 2010. "Grant will save 10 Peoria police officer jobs." *Journal Star* December 21. www.pjstar.com/news/x1882973274/Revised-grant-will-save-jobs-of-10-Peoria-police-officers.

PERF (Police Executive Research Forum). 2010. *Is the Economic Downturn Fundamentally Changing How We Police?* Critical Issues in Policing Series, vol. 16, Washington, D.C.: Police Executive Research Forum.

Rose, Elaine. 2010. "$1.1 million grant helps prevent layoffs for five Egg Harbor Township police officers." *Press of Atlantic City* September 30. www.pressofatlanticcity.com/news/press/atlantic/article_468eb94c-ccf9-11df-af56-001cc4c03286.html.

Shelly, Barbara. 2011. "Next chief has huge tasks waiting, and waiting…." *The Kansas City Star* September 15. www.kansascity.com/2011/09/15/3145454/next-chief-has-huge-task-waiting.html.

SNJCD (Southern New Jersey Development Council). 2011. "Countywide police force panel reviewing other options for Camden County." www.snjdc.org/2011/08/countywide-police-force-panel-reviewing-other-options-for-camden-county/.

Stelter, Leishen. 2011. "Police chief pushes partnerships: 'Fighting crime is a team sport.'" *United Publications, Inc.* June 21. www.securitydirectornews.com/?p=article&id=sd201106Z0AuM7

Trojanowicz, Robert, and Bonnie Bucqueroux. 1994. *Community Policing: How to Get Started.* Cincinnati, Ohio: Anderson Publishing Company.

USAonWatch. n.d. "Citizens on Patrol Volunteers Boost Texas County's Crime Preventions." www.usaonwatch.org/resource/publication.aspx?PublicationId=98.

VanHulle, Lindsay. 2011. "Lansing looks to merge police precincts." *www.lansingstatejournal.com* August 18. http://pqasb.pqarchiver.com/lansingstatejournal/access/2428604161.html?FMT=ABS&date=Aug+18%2C+2011.

Vedadi, Neena. 2011. "Volunteers Help Lighten the Load for Richland PD." *Fischer Interactive Network* September 12. www.keprtv.com/news/local/129695338.html.

Vijayan, Sunita. 2011. "Greenfield OKs deal to merge police force with Soledad's." *The California.com* September 14. www.thecalifornian.com/apps/pbcs.dll/article?AID=/201109140505/NEWS01/109140314.

Volunteers in Police Services. 2011a. "Origin of the Volunteers in Police Services (VIPS) Program." www.policevolunteers.org/about/.

Volunteers in Police Services. 2011b. "VIPS Registered Program Analysis Results." www.policevolunteers.org/cms/index.cfm?fa=detail&id=670.

Wexler, Chuck. 2010. "Survey Reveals Extent of Police Budget Cuts." PERF press release September 30. www.policeforum.org/dotAsset/36339.pdf

Wiseman, Jane. 2011. *Strategic Cutback Management: Law Enforcement Leadership for Lean Times.* Research for Practice, Washington, D.C.: U.S. Department of Justice, National Institute of Justice, NCJ 232077.

Zager, Matt. 2011. "Consolidations topic of federal budget forum." *The Daily Journal* June 22. www.thedailyjournal.com/article/20110622/NEWS01/106220326.